T0334132

Shaftesbury Road, Cambridge CB2 8EA, United Kingdom

One Liberty Plaza, 20th Floor, New York, NY 10006, USA

477 Williamstown Road, Port Melbourne, VIC 3207, Australia

314–321, 3rd Floor, Plot 3, Splendor Forum, Jasola District Centre,
New Delhi – 110025, India

103 Penang Road, #05–06/07, Visioncrest Commercial, Singapore 238467

Cambridge University Press is part of Cambridge University Press & Assessment,
a department of the University of Cambridge.

We share the University's mission to contribute to society through the pursuit of
education, learning and research at the highest international levels of excellence.

www.cambridge.org
Information on this title: www.cambridge.org/9781009507653

DOI: 10.1017/9781009238939

When citing this work, please include a reference to the DOI 10.1017/9781009238939

First published 2024

A catalogue record for this publication is available from the British Library.

ISBN 978-1-009-50765-3 Hardback
ISBN 978-1-009-23889-2 Paperback
ISSN 2633-9862 (online)
ISSN 2633-9854 (print)

Cambridge Elements ≡

Elements in Metaphysics
edited by
Tuomas E. Tahko
University of Bristol

METAPHYSICS
AND THE SCIENCES

Matteo Morganti
Roma Tre University

Metaphysics and the Sciences

Elements in Metaphysics

DOI: 10.1017/9781009238939
First published online: April 2024

Matteo Morganti
Roma Tre University

Author for correspondence: Matteo Morganti, matteo.morganti@uniroma3.it

Abstract: This Element presents and critically examines the relationship between metaphysics and the sciences. Section 1 provides a brief introduction. Section 2 looks at the methodological issues that arise when metaphysics and science get into contact, which is a much-debated aspect of the larger dispute concerning philosophical 'naturalism' and 'anti-naturalism'. A taxonomy of possible views is offered. Section 3 looks more specifically at milder forms of naturalism about metaphysics, which attempt in various ways to make it 'continuous' with science while preserving some degree of autonomy for it. Section 4 adds some reflections on what might be regarded as the most pressing open problem when it comes to doing scientifically oriented metaphysics (but also when practising metaphysics or science in isolation): the problem concerning theory choice and the value of non-empirical factors in determining which explanation of certain phenomena should be preferred.

Keywords: metaphysics, naturalism, science, theory choice, theoretical virtues

ISBNs: 9781009507653 (HB), 9781009238892 (PB), 9781009238939 (OC)
ISSNs: 2633-9862 (online), 2633-9854 (print)

Contents

Summary

This Element presents and critically examines the relationship between metaphysics and the sciences. Section 1 provides a brief introduction. Section 2 looks at the methodological issues that arise when metaphysics and science get into contact, which is a much-debated aspect of the larger dispute concerning philosophical 'naturalism' and 'anti-naturalism'. A taxonomy of possible views is offered. Section 3 looks more specifically at milder forms of naturalism about metaphysics, which attempt in various ways to make it 'continuous' with science while preserving some degree of autonomy for it. Section 4 adds some reflections on what might be regarded as the most pressing open problem when it comes to doing scientifically oriented metaphysics (but also when practising metaphysics or science in isolation): the problem concerning theory choice and the value of non-empirical factors in determining which explanation of certain phenomena should be preferred.

1 Introduction

Although there is no single shared definition, it is relatively uncontroversial to describe metaphysics as the study of reality based on the most general concepts and categories – reality being understood as broadly as possible, hence not limited to actually existing physical entities. As such, metaphysics investigates the nature of things intended in the widest sense (material objects, numbers, space, time, persons, propositions . . .), the features these possess or seem to possess (qualities, freedom, individuality . . .) and the relations that hold among them (causality, identity, truth-making . . .). In so doing, the metaphysician typically employs discipline-specific notions such as substance, trope, universal, essence, ontological dependence, grounding, fundamentality and the like, which are themselves subject to analysis.

Whether conceived as a 'top-down' enterprise starting from first-principles, or as a 'bottom-up' activity aiming to identify fundamental, general truths departing from particular matters of fact figuring as the initial explananda, metaphysics has traditionally been regarded as an activity based essentially on 'a priori' methods, that is, on reason alone, independently of the input coming from experience. More precisely, while it is not denied that experience loosely understood is the necessary point of departure for philosophical inquiry about the way things are (or could be), it has often been assumed in the past that metaphysicians go about formulating their hypotheses without seeking further support from the empirical domain: almost by definition, one could say, there is nothing like a metaphysical experiment.

Understood and practised along these lines, the metaphysical enterprise has long been firmly at the top of the hierarchy of human knowledge. This primacy, however, became progressively more problematic starting from the fifteenth to sixteenth centuries, and ultimately came under severe scrutiny in the last century or so. In particular, while it is undeniable that metaphysics and science have a common origin and share their historical development at least until the eighteenth to nineteenth centuries, in the last two centuries or so what was known as 'natural philosophy' has been steadily replaced by two distinct, and increasingly different, activities. Science and metaphysics appear today as sharply separated disciplines, not only with respect to their domains of application, questions and methodologies, but also in terms of their perceived relevance – science being almost inseparable from valuable technology and practical application, and metaphysics being regarded instead as irredeemably speculative and lacking actual usefulness. The origin of this process was, of course, the birth of modern science and the definition of a rigorous, and fruitful, scientific methodology of an essentially 'a posteriori' nature. Indeed, the ability of scientists to establish a systematic contact with reality through observation and experimentation, so lending a crucial factual support to the workings of reason, eventually led science to supersede natural philosophy by redefining its central goals and questions. In particular, the abovementioned aim of metaphysics, that of inquiring into the fundamental structure of reality in its most general features, was gradually replaced by something seemingly less ambitious, but at the same time much more tractable. Whereas metaphysicians have historically sought answers to big, allegedly fundamental interrogatives only to find that these systematically eluded them, one could say, scientists have instead identified manageable questions and realistic research aims in various fields, and regularly come up with productive ways of dealing with those questions and pursuing those aims.

To summarise the issue in the form of a (slightly strained) question, on what basis could one expect to discover something about reality by simply thinking about it, albeit in logically rigorous fashion, rather than by (also) directly interacting with it? The point becomes especially clear when it comes to philosophical inquiry that concerns things that are also dealt with by the sciences. Think about, for instance, the nature of space and time, or of material objects, or the origin of the universe. The thought certainly appears legitimate that in these cases the a priori methods of metaphysics had better leave room to the 'a posteriori' procedures of science, especially physics, which are based on abstract thinking but also, crucially, on observation and repeatable experiment. For, it seems undeniable that science turned out to be enormously more successful in providing answers to our questions about reality than metaphysics has ever been.

As a paradigmatic (albeit, again, deliberately tendentious) example, consider the following contrast between a typical metaphysical question (or set of questions) on the one hand, and a scientific one on the other. Material objects have properties, that is, qualitative aspects that we can get acquainted with through the senses, or with the help of instruments, or maybe only conjecture on the basis of experience. Now, starting at least with Plato, philosophers noticed that different objects sometimes share some of their properties, that is, bear qualitative similarities with one another. Based on this, they went on to concoct explanations for such similarities. Plato claimed that worldly things 'participate' in the natures of certain unchanging, perfect entities, called 'Forms', the separate existence of the latter making it possible for the former to exist as the sort of things they are, and to exemplify certain features to varying degrees. All horses, for instance, participate in the form 'Horsehood', which is the ground for their all being horses, similar to one another. Aristotle agreed with Plato on this but preferred to put these 'universal' forms directly into things rather than in a separate realm. Later philosophers continued to debate the issue, especially during the Middle Ages: some of them sided with Plato and/or Aristotle, perhaps modifying their theories in some detail. Others disagreed. So-called nominalists, in particular, denied that universals exist, and claimed that the universality of qualities is only a feature of our language, not of reality. The most radical among them rejected the idea of property altogether, arguing that only things exist, and their qualities – more precisely, the qualitative predicates that we use to talk about them – are a by-product of our classifications. Yet another group of nominalists proposed the hypothesis that properties exist, but they are not universals: rather, they are particular, non-repeatable 'tropes'. On this construal, every entity with some property P exemplifies its own specific P trope, and the similarity among all P tropes is a primitive fact, not determined by anything like a Form or a universal. Without venturing further into this so-called 'problem of universals', it should already appear clear that, interesting as they may be the various philosophical hypotheses as to the nature of properties that we just sketched do not seem to lend themselves to a discussion that can be significantly grounded (also) on empirical evidence – apart, obviously enough, from the very facts that constitute the relevant explananda.

Compare this with the development of elementary particle physics in the last century or so. After the shift from classical to quantum mechanics in the early twentieth century, physicists gradually came to agree on the fundamental description of the basic constituents of reality in terms of entities exhibiting both the characteristic features of particles and of waves, and exhaustively described by mathematical objects (called 'wavefunctions') that provide probabilistic information about their properties. After that, starting from the 1940s and 1950s, they progressively defined a coherent description of all particle types, the basic laws that govern them and their specific qualities. As for the latter, in particular, not only did the so-called Standard Model provide an elegant summary of all known particles; it also led to the successful prediction of the existence of more particles with specific properties. Indeed, the explanatory and predictive power of the Standard Model is one of the main reasons for physicists to take it seriously, and perhaps even to claim – as suggested by philosophers that endorse 'scientific realism' (more on this later) – that it is true or close to the truth about reality. Regardless of the issue of truth, at any rate, for present purposes it is sufficient to compare the generality and abstractness of the metaphysical debate about universals, and the complete lack of agreement about it among philosophers, on one side, and the level of success with which physicists have first conjectured and then discovered the properties of what are unanimously regarded nowadays as the fundamental constituents of reality, on the other. In spite of the fact that scientific hypotheses are in any case fallible and there are many important questions that remain open in contemporary elementary particle physics, the contrast between, so to put it, the metaphysics and the physics of fundamental properties should appear manifest. One could summarise it by saying that while scientists focus on the empirically tractable question 'Which properties are found in nature?', metaphysicians are interested in deeper, but much more abstract, questions having to do with the nature of properties themselves.[1]

In view of the foregoing, it is easy to see why, more often than not, reflection on the relationship between metaphysics and the sciences – a hotly debated topic nowadays, even though mostly if not exclusively among philosophers – tends to emphasise the differences and the potential conflict between them rather than to try to provide a picture of at least potential unity, convergence and complementarity. In a gradual but steady process, starting from the period of the scientific revolution and culminating in the central decades of the twentieth century, science has come to be regarded as a special, privileged activity: the systematic enterprise of gathering information about the world through observation and formulating testable hypotheses and full-blown theories on the basis of that information, so obtaining knowledge of the relevant domains in a way that is amenable to intersubjective check and systematic correction and improvement. This distinctive, and certainly

---

[1] As Maclaurin and Dyke put it, while '[s]cientists are interested in how various properties are distributed across the world [. . .] the question of what the metaphysical nature of properties is has no bearing whatsoever on the actual instances of properties out there in the world' (2012, 304). For a related discussion, concerning scientific and philosophical questions about laws of nature, see Hildebrand (2023, especially section 1).

virtuous, methodology has been put into contrast – by scientists but also philosophers – with that of philosophy, especially metaphysics. Beginning at least from the early twentieth century, the latter commenced to look like an activity which manifestly lacks a solid connection with reality, as well as clear procedural criteria and guiding principles. More generally, in stark comparison with the rigour and fecundity of science, metaphysics came to be regarded as almost completely detached from reality, and certainly short of well-defined standards of good practice. Especially within empiricist circles, as is well-known, science became a model, a paradigm that should ideally inform philosophy itself, promoting a change in the old ways of doing it and, if needed, the abandonment of at least some of them. In the case of philosophy as metaphysics, interpreted as seeking knowledge of the most fundamental and general facts about reality without having recourse to anything like an established and well-defined experimental methodology, it does not come as a surprise that – as recommended, in particular, by neopositivists in the first half of the twentieth century – it has often been regarded as an activity to be simply discontinued. As we will see in more detail in the next section, although metaphysics survived the neo-positivist campaign based on the thought that metaphysical questions are strictly meaningless, the idea that it has nothing to offer in addition to science is indeed alive and well. Putnam (2004), for instance, takes the question 'How many objects are there in a mini-world with exactly three point-particles?' to be a paradigmatic metaphysical question, and then attacks metaphysics by arguing that there is simply no way of tackling questions of this sort properly: after all, what could possibly give us an indication as to whether or not the sum of two things itself counts as 'one' (further) thing? In a similar vein, Van Fraassen (2002) discusses the question 'Does the world exist?' and ends up declaring that 'metaphysics is dead', as questions of this type may be endowed with meaning, but can only appear relevant from a very abstract, non-scientific perspective, and attempting to answer them is a waste of time. Other recent manifestations of this kind of scepticism towards traditional metaphysics include Ritchie (2008) and, less critically, Ladyman and Ross (2007). As we will see, some non-philosophers also joined enthusiastically the anti-metaphysics (in fact, in their case, anti-philosophy) camp. Something like the well-known Kantian point about those assertions that 'lay claim to insight into what is beyond the field of all possible experiences' [Critique of Pure Reason; A425/B453] is no doubt in the background here.

On the other hand, many thinkers in the more or less recent past adopted a symmetrically opposite stance, harshly criticising the idea that what is not amenable to scientific inquiry is in fact irrelevant if not meaningless.

Husserl, for instance (see Husserl 1970[1936]), famously argued that the development of modern science and technology led to a decline in Western culture, as it determined the inability to aptly engage with whatever does not present itself as an external object – that is, to interact with and get a grasp of the 'Lebenswelt', the fundamental domain of human experience is related to conscience, intentionality, etc. More generally, metaphysicians sometimes attempt a counterattack, and reject the key assumption according to which all questions about reality are best tackled based on the scientific method. The most radical among them go as far as to affirm the autonomy and priority of philosophy, especially metaphysics, and to consider science and the scientific method basically irrelevant for metaphysical inquiry (see Bealer 1996, 1998).

In between these two extremes – metaphysics dismissed in favour of science on the one hand, and metaphysics kept fully autonomous and prior to the sciences, on the other – several intermediate positions emerged, some of which constituted attempts at reconciliation and compromise between science and traditional metaphysical investigations. A well-known figure in this context is no doubt Wilfrid Sellars, who notoriously urged philosophers to seek some form of integration between the 'manifest image' of the world related to common sense and its 'scientific image', produced by scientific theorising (Sellars 1962). An important point to make in this context is a well-known Popperian one. As Popper pointed out, it is far from clear that a sharp demarcation can be identified between science and metaphysics. Moreover, to the extent that clear cases of scientific and metaphysical conjectures and theories can be identified, it is in any case plausible to think that extra-scientific, philosophical assumptions are routinely, and inevitably, made by practising scientists when they formulate their hypotheses. Following this route, proposals for a scientifically aware reformulation, rather than elimination, of metaphysics have been put forward more recently.

Faced with this complex net of interconnected problems and opposing perspectives, it is undoubtedly useful, if not necessary, for people interested in metaphysics to reflect carefully on its relationship (or lack thereof) with science. The present Element aims to help readers to do exactly this. Rather than by focusing on specific examples of metaphysics applied to science[2], or of the way in which science alone may, or may not, provide plausible answers to traditional philosophical problems, this will be done by keeping the discussion mostly at the general level, and proposing further reflections on the methodology and

---

[2] The label 'metaphysics of science' has become popular in recent years and is used to denote the philosophical study of genuinely philosophical concepts that turn out to play a key role in, or at least appear to be potentially relevant for, science in general as well as specific scientific disciplines and theories.

essential nature of the two activities. The first task will be (in Section 2) to present the various available views of metaphysics in connection to the sciences in as exhaustive, systematic and informative a way as possible. The guiding thread will be constituted by *naturalism* – which can be defined, at least at a first pass, as the request that non-science, in this case, philosophy as metaphysics, be made 'as continuous as possible' with the sciences.[3] Indeed, views on the methodology and content of metaphysics and its relationship with the sciences occupy a multiform spectrum going from 'extreme anti-naturalism' to radical, 'eliminative naturalism'. Our next step (in Section 3) will be to discuss in more detail the prospects for 'moderate' forms of naturalism, aiming, on the one side, to acknowledge the uniqueness of the methodology of science, which guarantees that our hypotheses and explanations always have the necessary anchoring to reality; and, on the other side, to preserve the ambitious nature of metaphysics as an enterprise the purpose of which is to define larger conceptual frameworks, tackle more general and deeper questions and provide the broadest possible understanding of the nature of things.

As we will see more clearly in the course of the discussion, a key point (if not THE key point) in one's assessment of metaphysics in connection with the sciences concerns explanation. To be sure, both metaphysics and the sciences aim to provide explanations of particular phenomena.[4] However, they do this in different ways, asking largely different questions and employing significantly different conceptual categories. This makes it natural to ask based on what criteria distinct, competing explanations should be critically assessed in science and in metaphysics, respectively, and when science and metaphysics meet. For reasons that will become clearer later, but essentially have to do with 'under-determination' (i.e., the fact that, at least in principle, there are always several competing explanatory hypotheses that are compatible with the available empirical data), the issue of theory choice crucially revolves around the role of extra-empirical factors and criteria in the assessment and evaluation of competing hypotheses and explanations. In the last section of this Element (Section 4), therefore, we will look at the dynamics of theory choice and the role of extra-empirical elements in metaphysics and in science.

While it was stated a moment ago that most of our discussion will move at a very general, mostly methodological level, it is no doubt useful to also zoom in

---

[3] Obviously enough, it is crucial to specify precisely what this continuity amounts to, and the amount of autonomy that should be acknowledged to metaphysics for it to become non-naturalistic. More on this later.

[4] This is by no means intended as a rigorous definition, of course. The aims of science, in particular, have been defined in rather different ways: scientific realists, for instance, would agree that science aims at the truth, while empiricists would instead claim that scientific theories have the function of accounting for and systematising known empirical data.

as much as possible and look at examples. For this reason, various points of the following sections of this Element will be devoted to the concise presentation and discussion of some sample disputes with respect to which both scientists and metaphysicians seem to have something relevant to say.[5]

2 Metaphysics and Science: A Taxonomy

As hinted at in the previous, introductory section, a fundamental issue that arises when one looks at metaphysics in connection to the sciences concerns its very credibility and usefulness as an autonomous discipline. Should we keep doing metaphysics given that science is so successful? Or is it reasonable to continue regarding metaphysics as more fundamental than, say, physics? Is there some way of establishing a fruitful interplay between the two? Several different answers to these questions, and consequently several philosophical positions concerning metaphysics and science, are available. These range from varieties of eliminativism and scepticism towards metaphysics that echo the dismissal recommended by the logical empiricists of the Vienna Circle, to the uncompromising denial of the view that empirical data and scientific theories may have an import on metaphysical theses, a priori tools of logical and conceptual analysis being autonomous with respect to, and more fundamental than, those that characterise scientific inquiry.

As mentioned, an attempt to present and discuss these views in a systematic fashion may usefully be based on the idea of naturalism. That is, the thought that philosophers should pay attention to the indications coming from the sciences, and philosophy as a discipline be made as continuous as possible with science. As already noted, talk of continuity (and discontinuity) between philosophy and the sciences is as widespread as irredeemably vague. Indeed, it allows for several nuances and, consequently, different forms of naturalism and anti-naturalism about metaphysics. To get things started, let us just assume for now the minimal sense of continuity according to which, whenever possible, the methodologies and results of the sciences should be taken into account by metaphysicians and be given some form of priority over those of traditional, a priori philosophical analysis.

It is important to emphasise that there are two components to this: a *methodological* component and an *ontological* component. With respect to the former, naturalists sometimes go as far as to recommend that metaphysics

---

[5] It is worth making explicit something that readers will have already noticed. Given that our focus here, as in most of – if not all – the recent literature on metaphysics, science and naturalism is on empirical knowledge, we will not consider case studies coming from non-empirical scientific disciplines such as mathematics or geometry. More generally, the discussion to follow will be concerned mostly if not exclusively with metaphysics in connection to the natural sciences.

itself turn into an empirical discipline, or else be discontinued; more often, they urge that metaphysics be practised in such a way that its claims are systematically provided with a solid empirical basis validated by science. With respect to the latter, naturalists insist instead that no ontological commitment should be made (if it is made at all!) unless it is grounded in scientific theorising. This may be intended in the sense that nothing should be said about what exists or does not exist if it is not read off directly from our best scientific theories; or, alternatively, in the sense that existential claims must always be in harmony with the indications coming from such theories, and possibly be instrumental to their further development and to an increase in our understanding of their content. Obviously enough, anti-naturalists reject both elements. More precisely, anti-naturalists about metaphysics believe that the latter is an autonomous field with a specific methodology which is largely different from, and independent of, the methodology of science; and that our ontological commitments need not be grounded in science, and may in fact even conflict with it if they deliver sufficient benefits in return – most likely, in terms of explanation.[6]

2.1 (Anti-)Naturalism, Scientific Realism and Physicalism

Two related themes are worth mentioning before starting our discussion. The first is *scientific realism*, that is, the issue concerning the epistemic value of scientific theories. Scientific realists believe that the best explanation for the success of science is that scientific theories are at least approximately true, and their truth content increases as new theories replace previous ones. Scientific antirealists, instead, believe either that scientific theories should not be taken literally as descriptions of things out there or, more commonly, that scientific theories should be understood literally but they are only true insofar as they make claims about the observable phenomena.[7]

Arguably, there is a direct link between scientific realism and naturalism about metaphysics. Indeed, many scientific realists are naturalists, in the sense that their high degree of trust in scientific theories, and their commitment to the

---

[6] Prima facie, it looks like one could be an anti-naturalist about methodology only or about ontological commitment only. Such a position, however, is arguably unstable: on what basis would someone be a methodological naturalist if not to put naturalistic restrictions on the sort of entities appearing in one's metaphysical hypotheses? And isn't naturalism about ontological commitment ultimately motivated by the assumption that the methodology of science constitutes a paradigmatic model of inquiry? On this latter point, see Emery's argument to the effect that those she calls 'content naturalists' should also be 'methodological naturalists' (Emery 2023, especially pp. 26–44).

[7] Sometimes (Van Fraassen 1980), scientific realism and anti-realism are formulated in terms of the aims of science. Here, however, we will stick to the formulation in terms of the (approximate) truth of current theories, which is more common as well as more convenient for our present purposes (see footnote 10 for a closely related point).

unobservable entities posited by those theories, is motivated at least in part by their belief that the scientific method is our best tool for uncovering the deep structure of reality. Consequently, it is this very same method that, they think, should be used as a guide in other domains. However, it is not necessary for a consistent naturalist to be a realist. A constructive empiricist such as Van Fraassen, for instance, would explicitly endorse the view that scientific theories only 'save the phenomena' and should not be taken literally when it comes to their claims about what is in principle not accessible to the senses (see Van Fraassen 1980). At the same time, constructive empiricists, and scientific antirealists more generally, (can) regard science as the most reliable source of rational belief about reality – and traditional metaphysics as lacking the same solid rational basis, hence as in need of naturalisation in the form of either reduction or elimination. On the other side of the spectrum, that anti-naturalism about metaphysics is coupled to scientific antirealism is clearly to be expected in some cases (e.g., those philosophical views according to which common sense and ordinary experience are to be given priority with respect to scientific hypotheses and beliefs); yet, the joint endorsement of scientific realism and anti-naturalism, perhaps motivated by the belief that there are other reliable sources of empirical knowledge *in addition to* the scientific method, is perfectly consistent. An example of the former attitude is Husserl, while the latter is arguably the view of authors such as E. J. Lowe – more on this shortly.[8]

An important, connected question is what epistemic attitudes naturalists can consistently have towards science and metaphysics, respectively. Define 'metaphysical realism' as the (indeed traditional) view that metaphysics seeks the truth and in at least some cases there are good reasons to think that metaphysical hypotheses provide (approximately) true descriptions of the fundamental structure of reality. The question is, then, what combinations of scientific (anti-)realism and metaphysical (anti-)realism are acceptable in a naturalistic context. Pending further discussion of metaphysical anti-realism in the final section of this Element, two remarks will suffice here. First, the combination of scientific anti-realism and metaphysical realism seems hard to justify in a naturalistic context: if one's ontological commitments should be constrained by science, and one's methodology cannot depart significantly from that of science, on what basis would one think that metaphysics uncovers the truth, but science does not? Secondly, one may suggest (Emery 2023) that, in view of the propounded continuity between science and metaphysics at the level of both content and methodology, a naturalist should either be a realist or an anti-realist about both science and metaphysics. A potential objection to this – in particular, in favour

---

[8] For an introduction to the debate about scientific realism, see Chakravartty (2017a).

of the viability of the combination of scientific realism and metaphysical anti-realism in a naturalistic context – is the following: in spite of the continuity between science and metaphysics, if there are good reasons at all for being scientific realists these do not have directly to do with scientific methodology; rather, they have to do with features that only characterise (some) scientific theories, but not metaphysical theories. These include the widespread agreement in the relevant community of researchers and, most notably, the ability to lead to unexpected novel predictions that turn out to be correct.

A related topic is *physicalism*. Physicalism is the thesis that everything that exists is ultimately physical or, slightly differently, that physical reality is the whole reality. One may think that, in order to settle the issue of naturalism versus anti-naturalism, one (just) has to settle the issue of physicalism. For, if one believes that everything is physical, then one is likely to also believe that our fundamental source of knowledge is science – primarily physics – and the other disciplines, especially metaphysics, should be made dependent on, or even reduced to, it. Moreover, it can be argued that the most credible form of naturalism is physicalism: for, even if one acknowledges the failure of strongly reductionist programmes in the philosophy of science such as that suggested by Oppenheim and Putnam (1958), there still seems to be an obvious way in which all other forms of inquiry depend on physics, as the latter is the discipline that deals with what is fundamental.[9] In the end, the issue of naturalism may even be thought to coincide with the issue of physicalism.

The above, however, is an incomplete and potentially misleading way of representing things. To begin with, a notorious problem exists concerning the exact definition of 'physical'. On a relaxed, 'negative' understanding, it just means 'non-mental'. On a more demanding construal, instead, it refers to whatever is explicitly posited by physical theory. Depending on which of these two alternatives is preferred for determining the exact content of the physicalist thesis, different consequences follow with respect to naturalism. On the strict sense of 'physical', for instance, physicalism seems to entail both ontological and methodological naturalism: for, if everything that exists

---

[9] That is to say, one could accept that the reduction of everything to physics is impossible, but at the same time insist that physicists deal with the most general laws of nature and study the basic structure of reality (at a level which can be deemed fundamental even independently of whether there is in fact an objective, ultimate layer of reality – for specific discussions of fundamentality in metaphysics and the sciences, see Tahko 2018 and Morganti 2020a, 2020b). It seems to be on the basis of something like this, for instance, that Ladyman and Ross (2007, 44) endorse their 'Primacy of Physics Constraint' in spite of their explicit rejection of the idea of a layered world with a fundamental level. According to the Primacy of Physics Constraint '[s]pecial science hypotheses that conflict with fundamental physics, or such consensus as there is in fundamental physics, should be rejected for that reason alone. Fundamental physical hypotheses are not symmetrically hostage to the conclusions of the special sciences'.

(at the fundamental level) is what physics says there is, the methods of physics and the ontological commitments implied by our best physical theories are all that matters. This conception of physicalism, however, gives rise to the infamous Hempel dilemma: are we talking about present physical theory, which is undeniably incomplete, or future physical theory, which is entirely unknown? Either way, if it doesn't become completely empty, the physicalist thesis certainly loses a lot if its appeal.[10] On the relaxed sense of 'physical', on the other hand, all positions seem to remain viable with respect to naturalism. For example, there might be reasons for believing that there are no non-mental things and yet not everything can be inquired into with the tools of (current) science, which would be a form of ontological naturalism (as physicalism) coupled with methodological anti-naturalism. Alternatively, one could contend that there may be more to reality than what is studied by physics, but any knowledge that we can hope to gain of it will come from science, that is, from scientific theories at one level or another. This would amount to the endorsement of a non-physicalist ontological naturalism together with a substantial from of methodological naturalism.

Notice, in this connection, that only the relaxed sense of 'physical' leaves room for the explanatory autonomy of the non-physical sciences – which is no doubt an important reason for the popularity in recent times of this understanding of physicalism and of the corresponding, non-reductive conception of naturalism. In more detail, if one is a physicalist in the strict sense then one is forced to believe that all the non-physical descriptions of parts of reality are in principle reducible to descriptions provided by present or future physics. However, this reductive, hierarchical view has been challenged many times and is definitely unpopular nowadays. The issue of multiple realisability can be usefully mentioned here. Particularly in the philosophy of mind, ambitious physicalist claims to the effect that every type of mental state, property or event corresponds to a precise type of physical state, property or event – to which it can consequently be reduced – have been rejected based on the strong evidence supporting the claim that mental states are multiply realised/realisable, that is, they (can) correspond to more than one physical counterpart. This seems a good reason for abandoning reductive physicalism: not surprisingly, most contemporary physicalists embrace 'non-reductive physicalism', that is, the view that the non-physical depends on, is grounded in, supervenes on, . . . the physical, yet does not reduce to it, hence the vocabulary of, say, psychology, is

---

[10] This is related to a worry voiced by McKenzie (2020): given that current science, especially physics, is arguably incomplete and even contains inconsistencies, naturalists about metaphysics should just sit and wait for a hypothetical 'final' theory. More on this in the final part of the present Element.

in principle not reducible to that of physics. Whatever one thinks about multiple realisability in the philosophy of mind, the point may carry over to metaphysics, 'intra-scientific' non-reducibility being stretched, as it were, with a view to defending the irreducibility of the metaphysical vocabulary and of metaphysical inquiry.

One final thought is that the issue concerning naturalism might not only be irreducible to the issue of physicalism, but also prior to it. For, granting that physicalism and its opposite can be formulated consistently, how could the truth of either be established entirely independently of every assumption about scientific versus non-scientific sources of knowledge? For sure, science can help in determining the precise content of the physicalist thesis – for example, by indicating in what sense and to what extent, if at all, the various empirical domains can be reduced to that of physics. However, belief in the truth or falsity of physicalism itself would remain largely untouched by this, as it seems to be ultimately based on prior – non-scientific – convictions and beliefs. Perhaps, all things considered, the right thing to say is that physicalism and naturalism (and, symmetrically, the denial of physicalism and anti-naturalism) are related but significantly independent theses which often go together as they are expressions of essentially the same basic philosophical inclination or 'stance'.[11]

2.2 Anti-naturalism

Let us get back now to our main theme. In the present context, *anti-naturalism* is the view that metaphysics need not worry about the indications coming from science, as there is no good reason for making the former in any way dependent on the latter – let alone for eliminating it in its favour.

Following the 'rationalist' tradition, for instance, some philosophers reject the idea that the truth about reality can be attained exclusively via a posteriori methods and believe instead that we should rely upon our ability to think and perform conceptual analyses, a significantly role being played in this context by intuition (see, e.g., Plantinga 2002 and Crisp 2016). Concerning this last point, that is, the recourse to intuition, it is worth emphasising that it is not easy to provide an uncontroversial definition. In fact, while the role of intuition in philosophy, especially metaphysics, is often discussed, it is not always clear what exactly the object of controversy is, and whether intuition is intended in essentially the same way by all parties. A person S may be said to have an

---

[11] A stance being a favourable propositional attitude weaker than belief in that something is 'accepted' yet not regarded as true. More generally, a stance can be intended as a basic perspective on the world, which is a starting point for generating hypotheses and beliefs. See Van Fraassen (2002), and Chakravartty (2017). We will return to this idea a few times in what follows. For specific discussions of physicalism and naturalism, see Kim (2011) and Witmer (2012). For a general introduction and overview, Stoljar (2023).

intuition that x at a time t, if it seems to S that x at t based on the beliefs that S entertains at t (in particular, the most entrenched beliefs based on perception and common sense). In this sense, however, intuition does not seem to be particularly problematic, and may even be regarded as a necessary starting point for updating one's belief system. There is of course an issue concerning the weight one should attribute to intuitive beliefs and the extent and criteria based on which one should revise one's current beliefs, or stick to them, when faced with reasons (say, related to a successful scientific theory that departs decidedly from common sense) for doing otherwise. This issue, however, does not concern intuition per se. On this construal of intuition, as a matter of fact, naturalists can be perfectly happy to accept it as one of the elements to be taken into account when devising and evaluating explanatory hypotheses – even if only for contrasting intuitively held beliefs with beliefs of a different nature, and/or examining their cognitive/psychological grounds and underlying mechanisms. A much more controversial sense of intuition, and one that seems much more problematic for the naturalist, is the sense according to which intuition constitutes a sui generis source of belief and justification. Taking their cue from 'epistemological rationalism', the view that at least some beliefs are justified, but not on the basis of inner or outer experience (Bonjour 1998), anti-naturalists may claim that 'rational intuition' is an irreducible and largely independent cognitive faculty. As such, they may add, intuition is at the basis of philosophy and metaphysics, and makes them prior to, or at least largely autonomous from, science and empirical inquiry more generally (Bealer 1998).[12]

Other anti-naturalists make a claim about the scope of metaphysics rather than the source of justification for our beliefs. Some authors, in particular, acknowledge the value of scientific hypotheses, and even that science should be taken seriously by philosophers as it provides potential access to empirical truths about some specific domains. Yet, they claim, scientific knowledge is in principle more limited than metaphysical knowledge, hence should be integrated by, and subordinated to, the latter. According to Lowe (2011), for example, metaphysics explores a space of possibilities a definition of which is a sort of necessary precondition for scientific inquiry, which deals 'only' with what is actual (or, at any rate, with a much more restricted sense of possibility).[13] Defending the a priori nature of metaphysics,

---

[12] For a general discussion of intuition in philosophy, see Pust (2019). See also DePaul and Ramsey (1998), Kornblith (1998) and Pust (2000).

[13] We will get back to this point later, but it is worth getting rid of a potential ambiguity straightaway. While metaphysicians may be interested in studying what is possible, necessary and/or impossible, and even the very nature of modality, people like Lowe (see also Morganti and Tahko 2017) seem to have in mind something different. Namely, that metaphysicians put forward various explanatory hypotheses that they regard as possible ways the world could be, to be then further evaluated based on the indications coming from science.

people like Hudson (2016) contend instead that metaphysics employs tools, including intuition, which are in fact present in science as well. Hence the methodology of metaphysics cannot be considered less reliable than scientific methodology merely because the latter is more focused on the input of experience. Indeed, says Hudson, metaphysics allows for a broader range of explanantia than the sciences, and it consequently becomes practicable – in fact, necessary – when, as it seems inevitable, scientific research reaches the point where it cannot but stop seeking further explanations.

Thus, anti-naturalism about metaphysics is not so much a claim about the *complete autonomy* of philosophical inquiry. Rather, it is essentially the view that there is no sense in which science should be given any priority outside of its specific domain: in fact, the methods of a priori metaphysics have the potential to uncover deeper and more general truths about reality.[14]

Among anti-naturalists, a further differentiation can be made, dividing them in two groups. On the one hand, there are those who give priority to common sense and the manifest image of the world and, consequently, to the task of providing explanations of the way reality appears to us in our everyday life. In connection to this, we already mentioned Husserl and Sellars in the introduction. Peter Strawson's 'descriptive metaphysics' (1959) is also an example of this attitude, as well as the philosophy of G.E. Moore (see Moore 1959, especially the essays *A Defence of Common Sense* and *Proof of an External World*).[15] On the other hand, there are philosophers (E.J. Lowe, for instance, arguably being one of them) who are happy to critically assess the manifest image of the world, and possibly revise it to some extent, but insist that, in so doing, metaphysical inquiry comes first, as it is prior to the sciences in terms of generality and depth.

What about the naturalistic side of the divide?

2.3 Naturalism

A useful starting point here is constituted by the views of Carnap and Quine on philosophical methodology and ontological commitment, that is, what we

---

[14] It is of course entirely possible to conceive of anti-naturalism about metaphysics as a claim of complete autonomy. This position, however, is rarely if ever endorsed nowadays. That most contemporary metaphysicians are naturalists in the sense that they do not accept metaphysical theories that conflict with the content of our best scientific theories is convincingly argued by Emery (2023, especially chapter 1).

[15] One may object that Moore and Strawson are naturalists, in that they consider empirical facts about humans and their environment as a fundamental starting point. However, in their philosophical systems this attitude is not accompanied by the emphasis on science and scientific knowledge that we are assuming to be essential for naturalism here. Strawson, for instance, rather than seeking the input of the empirical sciences, proceeds on the basis of 'transcendental arguments': that is, arguments of an a priori nature that infer conclusions about what the world must be like from the identification of the fundamental features of our ways of thinking about it in our day-to-day experience.

should think exists and on what grounds. Besides revealing some important motivations underlying naturalism, a brief illustration of the opinions held on these matters by Carnap and Quine will also allow us to further elaborate upon the distinction, introduced at the beginning of this section, between methodological naturalism and ontological naturalism.

Carnap was a member of the Vienna Circle, which we mentioned already in the introduction. In his opinion, and in that of other 'logical positivists' (also called 'logical empiricists', or 'neo-positivists'), philosophy should steer clear of what he named 'pseudo-problems'. That is, problems that are formulated in terms of concepts that purport to refer to the world, but in fact have no significant empirical implications whatsoever (see Carnap 1967). The basic reason for this belief has to do with one of the key assumptions of logical positivism: the principle of verification. According to it, the meaning of a statement coincides with the method of its verification via empirical means. In the opinion of Carnap and other logical positivists, since metaphysical statements cannot be verified – in particular, a way of checking whether they are true or false based on experience seems to be unavailable in principle – one must conclude that metaphysics is meaningless and should be discontinued. Carnap, therefore, expressed concerns about metaphysics that are essentially *semantic*.[16] More generally, based on the assumption that all meaningful statements are either logical or empirically verifiable, and science provides the best grounds for formulating justified empirical statements, logical positivists believed that philosophy should be turned into the rigorous analysis of the logical foundations of scientific knowledge. One consequence of this is that existential commitment should only be made within a specific linguistic/conceptual scientific framework (Carnap 1950). In particular, whether something exists is a question that can only be given a plausible answer from the vantage point of a specific scientific theory. Internally to a particular scientific theory, though, an ontology is defined almost automatically: for, accepting such a theory consists (among other things) in saying that there are certain entities with such and such properties. The price of this 'dissolution' of ontological issues is, of course, that it makes sense to talk about reality only within the perspective of particular scientific constructions. This defines a peculiar 'empirical realism' which is arguably weaker than traditional scientific realism (see above) in that ontological commitment is always relative to a theoretical framework (as an answer to an 'internal question' raised in relation to such framework) and not to be intended in an absolute sense

---

[16] The principle of verification was by no means uncontroversial. Logical positivists disagreed over its exact formulation (should verification be something that can be actually carried out?) and then, primarily due to the fact that inductive generalisations are in principle unverifiable, replaced it with criteria based on controllability and confirmability.

(as an answer to an 'external question' concerning what 'really' exists, independently of any theory). In this context, to repeat the key point, there is no work left for the metaphysician: doing metaphysics, according to Carnap, would mean to hopelessly attempt to formulate and answer existential questions from outside all respectable theoretical frameworks, employing concepts that are ultimately meaningless.

The foregoing resonates with Quine's (see, e.g., Quine 1981) overt endorsement of naturalism based on the firm belief that there is no higher tribunal for truth than natural science and philosophy is (or at least should be intended as) itself an empirical science. For Quine too, existential commitment should follow from a careful examination of the entities that are postulated by scientific theories (Quine 1951). In particular, answers to existential questions have to be sought on the basis of our best current scientific theories in the relevant domains, with the simple addition of the appropriate tools for their formal regimentation and considerations of (in)dispensability of the relevant entities. Importantly, though, for Quine the ensuing conclusions can be regarded as valid in general, that is, not only internally to a particular framework. This opens up some space for interpretation – indeed, the interpretation of Quine's view on these matters is by no means uncontroversial. On the one hand, the foregoing can be considered instrumental to the endorsement by Quine of a sort of deflationism about metaphysics that was even more radical than Carnap's, in the sense that Quine was an empirical realist like Carnap but rejected the very idea of an external framework.[17] On the other hand, the amount of work done by Quine with a view to answering existential questions and clarifying the nature of various kinds of entities may well justify a less radical reading in terms of 'non-eliminative' naturalism about metaphysics.[18] Be this as it may, Quine's emphasis on ontology, as well as some of his methodological considerations (e.g., about indispensability) are arguably present in later metaphysics.[19]

---

[17] See Quine (1981, 21–22), Hylton (1994, 267) and Price (2007, 393). On Carnap and Quine on ontology, see Alspector-Kelly (2001).

[18] This ambiguity may be due at least in part to the fact that Quine never formulated general theories of knowledge and meaningfulness that could lead him to a systematic, explicit rejection of metaphysics (see Rosen 2014).

[19] In relation to this, it is interesting to note that it is more or less explicitly in contrast with a 'neo-Quinean' approach to metaphysics that some practising metaphysicians have characterised their discipline lately. Lowe (2011), for instance, distinguishes between bad metaphysics, aiming to provide a list of existing kind of things, and good metaphysics, which deals instead with fundamental categories and possibilities. On a similar note, Schaffer (2009) agrees with the Carnapian/Quinean view that most, if not all, relevant existential questions find immediate answers within the relevant scientific theories. However, he also argues, what exists is not the issue but rather the starting point, metaphysics being primarily (as per the 'neo-Aristotelian' approach to the discipline) a study of the way in which the structure of the world is determined by priority and dependence relations.

One may regard as (unknowing) recent examples of the radical, eliminative form of naturalism endorsed by Carnap and (at least on some readings) Quine famous physicists who openly declared, in various occasions, that philosophy is dead: among them, Stephen Hawking, Lawrence Krauss and Neil DeGrasse Tyson. The belief shared by these scientists is that physics has proven to be able to turn issues that philosophers have debated for centuries without reaching any sort of result – or even just a significant agreement – into empirically manageable questions. Hence, philosophy (including metaphysics) should be abandoned in favour of the hard sciences once and for all. It could be objected that most, if not all, non-philosophers who are eliminativists about metaphysics (and philosophy more generally) do not have a genuine appreciation of the nature of contemporary philosophy. This may well be. However, there are several philosophers who certainly have a good grasp of what metaphysical inquiry amounts to and yet, even long after the decline of logical positivism, endorse this radical viewpoint with respect to metaphysics. An eliminativist perspective can, for example, be attributed to Van Fraassen and the late Putnam, whom we mentioned in the introduction. In the work of these authors, the concern with metaphysics seems to have become *epistemic* rather than semantic as in the case of Carnap and the logical positivists. That is, metaphysical claims are regarded as (at least in some cases) meaningful, yet metaphysical hypotheses are discarded nonetheless because of their systematic lack of the necessary degree of 'epistemic credibility'.[20]

Another approach that it seems fitting to include here is the programme for the naturalisation of metaphysics put forward by Goldman (2007, 2015, see also Goldman and McLaughlin 2019): a sort of 'experimental metaphysics' (Rose 2017) aiming to analyse entrenched metaphysical categories – such as, for instance, those of event, causation or individual – by employing the tools of psychology and the cognitive sciences. In the case of events, for example, Goldman (2007) presents empirical evidence in support of a 'compromise position' with respect to their individuation. While 'unifiers' believe that, say, Oliver's saying 'I apologise' and his apologising are one and the same event, 'multipliers' disagree based on the fact that the two events have different constituents. Shifting from ontology to the analysis of our mental representations, Goldman argues, makes it possible to sidestep the ontological question

---

[20] The distinction between semantic and epistemic concerns about metaphysics is probably not sharp: after all, the claim that questions such as 'How many objects exist in a mini-world with three point-particles?' are meaningful but lack possible answering strategies as a matter of principle; and the claim that they are meaningless because they violate something like a principle of verification are remarkably close. Plausibly, the exact way in which the divide is drawn co-varies with one's semantics. At any rate, nothing hinges on this in what follows.

and point out instead that our representations work in some cases in agreement with the views of unifiers, and in some other cases in a way that follows the multipliers' theory. This sort of approach qualifies as a form of naturalism exactly because it is essentially based on science and the empirical study of our conceptual categories as they are employed at the level of everyday experience and common sense. Clearly, though, in this case naturalisation does not imply elimination only because it leads to a radical reconceptualisation, in fact a replacement, of metaphysics as it is traditionally conceived. Equally clearly, on this construal several traditional questions of metaphysics, lacking the necessary anchoring in our everyday use of the corresponding concepts, are nonetheless dismissed.[21]

A less radical form of naturalism about metaphysics is what one may refer to as *strongly reductive naturalism*. In this case, metaphysics is not regarded as pointless based on semantic and/or epistemic concerns, but rather as something that should be strongly constrained through a serious and systematic reference, and deference, to scientific methodology and scientific theories.

A philosopher who can plausibly be characterised as a strongly reductive naturalist about metaphysics is Penelope Maddy. Maddy recommends what she calls 'second philosophy', a way of doing philosophy that she regards as a radical and austere form of naturalism, and that consists in steering clear of the big philosophical questions and systems, having recourse instead to 'what we typically describe with our rough and ready term "scientific method"' (2007, 2). The second philosopher is not interested in the issue of demarcating metaphysics from science, nor in putting forward general claims. Rather, she deals with ontological questions on a piecemeal basis, and 'though she is motivated by purely scientific concerns and employs purely scientific methods, she ends up deliberating effectively on traditional metaphysical questions [. . ..] The Second Philosopher conducts her metaphysical inquiry as she does every other inquiry, beginning with observation, experimentation, theory formation and testing, refining and revising as she goes' (Maddy 2007, 410–411). The foregoing, together with the examples she offers (which concern, for instance, the nature of mathematical entities, but also the reality of atoms and the electro-magnetic fields) – as well as her explicit discussion of Quine and his tradition – clearly show that Maddy exemplifies the non-eliminative version of naturalism about metaphysics.

Another paradigmatic approach is the proposal put forward by Ladyman and Ross (2007). According to these authors, traditional analytic metaphysics (in

---

[21] In this area of research, it is worth mentioning the study, based on the examination of folk judgments about certain type of cognitive scenarios, of metaphysical explanation as it appears in ordinary contexts, presented in Miller and Norton (2022).

Ladyman and Ross's terminology, 'neo-Scholastic metaphysics') should be dismissed because it is based on an a priori methodology that is insufficient for forming reasonably justified beliefs about reality – the main concern thus being once again epistemic rather than semantic.[22] Ladyman and Ross concede that many metaphysicians are aware that our ordinary, everyday beliefs (together with conceptual analysis) may not be enough to make bold claims as to the ultimate nature of reality, and one should consequently pay attention to the indications coming from science. Nonetheless, they argue, what most neo-Scholastic metaphysicians do is carry out their work referring in non-systematic fashion to putative scientific claims and scenarios that in any case qualify – at best – as 'A-level chemistry'. At the same time, common sense and intuition are often used as guides for adjudicating among different theoretical alternatives.[23] According to Ladyman and Ross, there is no reason for thinking that the results of this sort of activity are of any real value.[24]

In terms of their positive proposal, Ladyman and Ross recommend doing metaphysics on the basis of a genuine knowledge of the most recent developments of science, especially physics. Indeed, they endorse a 'Principle of Naturalistic Closure', based on which one should deem acceptable only general metaphysical hypotheses that serve to unify our best current physics with another scientific hypothesis (although it is not explicitly stated, this is likely to include the unification of separate parts of our best current physics). Unification is intended here in the sense that two or more specific scientific hypotheses, at least one of which is drawn from fundamental physics, jointly explain more than the sum of what is explained by the two hypotheses taken separately. Ladyman and Ross's favourite example is the notion of structure. According to them, an ontologically loaded conception of relational structure allegedly provides a unified metaphysical underpinning to a vast range of facts having to do with continuity across theory-change in the history of science, the peculiarities of quantum physics and general relativity, the usefulness of the notion of an 'information pattern' and more.

---

[22] Ladyman, for instance, summarises his take on naturalised metaphysicians and traditional metaphysical questions by stating that 'it is clear that they regard some of those questions as meaningful, but as making insufficient contact with reality to be worth entertaining' (Ladyman 2017, 143).

[23] Getting back to the earlier discussion of intuition, Ladyman and Ross do not attribute to neo-Scholastic metaphysicians the idea that there is a special faculty that lends non-empirical justification to our claims about reality. Rather, they refer to the weight that these metaphysicians ascribe to seemings based on ordinary experience. The seemings and beliefs that have this origin, they note, are the by-product of evolution. As such, useful as they may be, they are not a good guide when it comes to hypotheses that go beyond common sense and observable macroscopic phenomena.

[24] For other critiques of 'free-range', unconstrained, non-naturalistic metaphysics, see Bryant (2020) and Maclaurin and Dyke (2012). For an interesting response to the latter, see McLeod and Parsons (2013).

Although his specifically metaphysical claims are different, Maudlin (2007) similarly recommends the dissolution of metaphysics into the special sciences, again giving centre stage to contemporary physics.

Perhaps less well-known is the conception of 'experimental metaphysics' in the sense originally proposed by Shimony (1981). According to Shimony, contemporary science – once more, physics in particular – managed to make metaphysics experimental. For, it enabled us to test empirically the consequences of at least some metaphysical hypotheses. Shimony's favourite example concerns the notion of *locality* – that is, the idea that there can be no immediate influence on a physical system by another physical system which is distinct, and at some distance, from it, as every interaction must be mediated – as per the theory of relativity – at a speed smaller than or equal to the speed of light. Indeed, quantum mechanics seems to imply a direct empirical falsification of locality, as certain quantum systems (so-called 'entangled' systems) are such that the determination of the properties of one of them appears to immediately 'affect' the properties of another. This alleged empirical refutation of the hypothesis of locality by quantum mechanics is taken by Shimony to exemplify a more general dynamics. Indeed, he recommends the use of *modus tollens* in the following way: a given metaphysical hypothesis MH may imply a consequence C about the world, and observation based on physical theory may indicate that C is false. As a result, MH can be deemed false as well. The foregoing can be understood along essentially Popperian lines: regardless of where a general hypothesis about reality comes from, if experience refutes a consequence that can be deductively inferred from it, then we should conclude that the hypothesis in question has been conclusively shown to be false. In the case of locality and quantum mechanics, says Shimony, physics has taught us that a certain metaphysical hypothesis is false and physical interactions may violate locality. Such a result appears of course quite relevant for naturalistic philosophers: if Shimony is right, then the naturalisation of metaphysics might be based on a clear, simple methodology that makes it possible to perform 'empirical tests' also in the case of metaphysical hypotheses. From this perspective, by looking at the various domains of empirical inquiry one may hope to find compelling indications that, as science progresses, several typically metaphysical questions, concerning for instance the nature of time and space, or the notion of an individual material object, become potential subjects of empirical inquiry – at least in the sense that certain hypotheses are shown to be unworkable based on the available evidence.[25]

---

[25] It is an open question whether this amounts to making metaphysics continuous with science without eliminating it, or rather to naturalisation as elimination/replacement. Note the similarity between this approach and the form of eliminativism explicitly endorsed by physicists such as Hawking, Krauss and DeGrasse Tyson, mentioned earlier.

On the other end of the naturalist spectrum, one finds the approach that has come to be known as the 'Canberra Plan'. This is the view that the best way to implement philosophical naturalism is to first perform conceptual analysis in the traditional a priori fashion, and then seek ways to harmonise the results of this procedure with the indications coming from the sciences, so warranting a strong empirical basis for our philosophy. Typically, a Canberra planner starts from the entities that we quantify over in our ordinary discourse, and the platitudes believed by most or all competent speakers concerning the topic at hand. The outcome of the investigation has the form of a 'Ramsey sentence' – that is, of an existentially quantified sentence that describes the entity in question without mentioning it explicitly. While in principle this method could give a priori results (in case the assembled platitudes are regarded as *defining* the theoretical term in question), the role-fillers are normally sought with the help of the sciences whenever possible – most philosophers belonging to this group are self-proclaimed naturalists, as well as physicalists. Inspired in different ways by the work of Armstrong, Lewis and Jackson, this methodology has recently become quite popular (see Braddon-Mitchell and Nola 2009).

2.4 Overview and Discussion

Faced with all these alternatives and their diverse assumptions, it seems hard to determine which form of naturalism, or anti-naturalism, should be preferred and why. Luckily, it is not necessary to attempt a conclusive assessment here. Pending further discussion – in particular, of putatively intermediate, 'mildly naturalistic' views – in the next section, let us now summarise the preceding presentation of the main options.

It is perhaps useful to say a bit more about this taxonomy on the basis of a couple of sample metaphysical issues.

2.4.1 Fundamentalia

Consider first the question concerning the fundamental categories of being, that is, the fundamental kinds of entities that constitute reality. Undeniably, the quest for these alleged fundamentalia has been a distinctive feature of Western philosophy since its inception, with different thinkers variously regarding as fundamental familiar elements such as water or fire, the infinite/indefinite, atoms or even infinitely divisible 'seeds'. What do contemporary metaphysicians think about this issue? Let us provide a general (and necessarily generic) answer following the different methodological approaches described in the preceding pages, schematised in Table 1 below.

Table 1 Possible views of metaphysics in its relationship with the sciences, going from radical anti-naturalism (left) to radical naturalism (right).

Anti-naturalism						Naturalism
The a priori methods of metaphysics, possibly including a sui generis form of intuition, can uncover the truth, perhaps even in domains that are inquired into by the sciences (e.g., Bealer, Plantinga, Crisp)	A priori metaphysics comes first, as it accounts for common sense, that is, ordinary, non-scientific facts (e.g., Strawson's descriptive metaphysics)	Although it should engage with the sciences as much as possible, a priori metaphysics identifies possible ways things could be like, prior to scientific inquiry (e.g., Lowe)	A priori conceptual analysis should be performed first, based on ordinary experience; scientific knowledge is, however, then required as a fundamental 'testing ground' (e.g., Canberra Plan)	Metaphysics should be derived directly from science (scientifically based ontological investigations – for example, Maddy; potential falsification of hypotheses – for example, Shimony; unification of scientific hypotheses – for example, Ladyman and Ross)	Metaphysics should itself turn into a purely a posteriori enterprise (e.g., Goldman)	Metaphysics should be dismissed (e.g., Carnap, Putnam, Van Fraassen)

According to the stronger forms of anti-naturalism, regardless of the epistemic value of science, a priori reflection – possibly on the basis of a sui generis faculty of intuition – can lead us to identify basic truths about the ultimate structure of things. For instance, that reality must be composed of Aristotelian substances, as only these can account for identity, unity, persistence and change.

Descriptive metaphysicians à la Strawson would instead start from the observation that we conceptualise the world in certain ways to conclude on the basis of transcendental reasoning that, say, it must include individual objects (Strawson 1959).

Others would admit that there are several possible accounts of the fundamental – the identification of which is an exclusive aim of metaphysics. Based on this, however, they would then go on to pick one particular view based on its overall explanatory power – which may include the ability to fit with our best scientific theories but does not necessarily have that as a primary aim. Lowe (2007), for instance, puts forward a four-category ontology of substantial and non-substantial particulars and substantial and non-substantial universals, whose explanatory power he takes to largely compensate its lack of economy with respect to other philosophical systems. It is this four-category ontology, says Lowe, which should be used as a 'metaphysical foundation for natural science'.

What a Canberra planner would typically do is again something different: based on conceptual analysis, they would first describe our typical conception of, say, what being an object amounts to.[26] Crucially, they would then turn to our best knowledge of the natural world, hence science, to test that description. In this case, while the test would be passed in the case of classical physics, quantum physics would entail that there is nothing corresponding to our conception, at least not at the fundamental level. This would entail the partial falsification, hence the need for revision, of our common sense conception of object hood.

As for the stronger forms of naturalism, an experimental metaphysician in Goldman's and Rose's sense (see above, pp. 18–19) would only be interested in the origin and structural features of our ways of conceptualising the world, so essentially focusing exclusively on something like the first part of the strategy endorsed by proponents of the Canberra plan. Other forms of radical naturalism would instead go straight to science, as it were, seeking a clear answer to the initial question – if it can be found at all – directly in the best available theories. As mentioned, for instance, Ladyman and Ross (2007) examine contemporary physics

---

[26] Philosophers of this group are normally interested in more complex notions such as meaning or the mind, but this is immaterial here.

and conclude that it gives us good reasons for thinking that the fundamental category is that of relational structure.[27]

Lastly, eliminative naturalists would of course reject the very use of philosophical categories such as, say, substance, object or universal, and answer the initial question in the language of science itself – consequently stating, for instance, that what is fundamental are the elementary particles of the Standard Model (together perhaps with other things equally certified by the sciences), and nothing else can be usefully added to this.[28]

2.4.2 The Notion of Natural Kind between Metaphysics, Biology and More

Next, let us look at natural kinds. That there are kinds of things sharing a common nature is a widespread, entrenched belief. Several philosophers held it, often taking the fact that certain entities are members of the same kind to be the ground for the fact that these entities support our inductive inferences and talk about laws of nature (an example of this being J.S. Mill). For these realists about natural kinds, the question then arises as to their metaphysical status. Views about this vary and span a spectrum going from primitivism – natural kinds are fundamental and not reducible to any other category – to the conception of natural kinds as universals, to their reduction to groups of properties, in particular natural (perhaps, also essential) properties. Other philosophers, however, object to the idea of there being objective divisions of this sort in reality. According to them, kinds are not natural, but rather conventional entities. On weaker forms of conventionalism, expressed for instance by empiricists such as Locke, there might well be real essences and kinds, but we are not – and will never be – in a position to identify them, or at least to be able to tell when this happens.

Against the background just sketched, how could philosophers try to make progress on the topic of natural kinds?[29] Besides further refining the relevant notions and working categories, a useful thing to do, as illustrated for instance by Bird and Tobin (2023), is to look at the application of the notion of natural kind in the specific sciences.

---

[27] It must be mentioned that this notion of fundamental structure and fundamental category need not be paired with the idea that there is (or even, must be) a fundamental 'level' or 'layer' to reality. Indeed, Ladyman and Ross explicitly reject talk of fundamentality in this latter sense – again on the basis of the indications they take to be provided by physics.

[28] Non-eliminative naturalism of the broadly Quinean type (see the earlier discussions of Maddy and of Quine himself) would differ only in that it avoids the explicit rejection of metaphysics as a discipline and the explicit restriction of the validity of ontological claims to specific linguistic/theoretical frameworks.

[29] A useful, book-length assessment is provided by Khalidi (2013).

In physics, it is relatively uncontroversial that there are natural kinds in the traditional, intuitive sense: elementary particles, for instance, are unambiguously divided into different types based on their essential features.

In chemistry, however, things are already less clear-cut: while elements can be identified based on their atomic number, hence their elementary parts, when it comes to compounds it is possible that distinct types of things have the same constituents. It follows that the way in which certain components are arranged also contributes to the definition of the relevant kinds. Perhaps more importantly, macroscopic substances can be identified with specific chemical structures only loosely: for instance, virtually any sample of water contains positive and negative ions in addition to instances of the familiar, neutral structure of two hydrogen atoms and one oxygen atom. Therefore, it is not strictly speaking true that 'water is H_2O'. Moreover, more complex molecules, such as proteins, are in many cases categorised based on their function rather than on their internal composition, putting further limits on the efficacy of the above 'microstructuralist' view of chemical kinds.

Moving to biology, it is a fact that practising scientists classify species in different, incompatible ways – based on common ancestry, interbreeding and/or qualitative similarity. The question thus arises whether some form of natural kind pluralism/weak conventionalism is appropriate for biology; or it is instead advisable to insist on the existence of the 'right' way of classifying; or, alternatively, accept eliminativism about natural kinds in this specific context. It is basically with biology in mind that Boyd (1999) introduced the 'homeostatic cluster' conception of natural kinds. According to it, there are mechanisms of some sort that make it the case that certain properties tend to group together. Crucially, the resulting clusters need not include any property by necessity – which makes the view flexible enough to avoid the limits of other accounts (in particular, essentialism) and be applicable to biological species and similar categories.

In connection to this, a particularly interesting domain is that of psychiatry. Unlike what happens for (most) biological diseases, caused by specific viruses or bacteria and normally leading to well defined symptoms, psychiatric conditions are much harder to classify based on their causes and manifestations. While, for several years now, attempts have been made to compile exhaustive 'handbooks' – the notorious 'Diagnostic and Statistical Manual of Mental Disorders' of the American Psychiatry Association – there is a consensus among philosophers that the resulting classifications are significantly arbitrary. Mental conditions are hard to classify, and even on a cluster view of kinds they often escape categorisation – in particular, because they generally lack a well-defined underlying mechanism, causing the exemplification of certain properties. All things considered, a form of 'promiscuous realism' (Duprè 1993) – the view that there are many different and equally respectable taxonomies, as the world is complex and lends itself to several ways of categorising it – might be the way to go in this case; or even a more radical antirealist and eliminativist perspective such as that recommended, for instance, by Hacking (2007).[30]

Things are similarly complex in other domains. In psychology, for instance, attempting to answer the question whether mental states form natural kinds seems to require a prior decision with respect to nothing less than the mind-body problem. As for the social sciences, it seems quite clear there that classification is dependent on human interests and aims and, moreover, the very act of classification has, or may have, repercussions on its objects – which are themselves human beings with certain expectations, aims and self-images, and who consequently are likely to react to being classified. Consider in this connection the concept of race. Historically, the idea of race emerged quite naturally from the observation of the undeniable differences that exist among different human groups. As such, it was immediately connected to some hypothetical biological ground, taken to be the cause of the traits that were manifested by certain individuals and inherited by their offspring. A corresponding 'scientific' classification emerged in the modern era, in parallel with the growing interest in taxonomy in other fields, especially biology. For quite some time, the notion was taken for granted, the debate essentially focusing on whether all races descended from common ancestors – 'monogenesis' – or several distinct ancestors had to be postulated – 'polygenesis'. With the work of Darwin, monogenesis gained the upper hand, together with the idea that sexual selection determines the creation and stabilisation of racial groups. From this, the focus then shifted – rather sadly – to the idea of controlling the evolution of races via active human intervention (the so-called 'eugenics' of Galton). The notion of race, however, subsequently came under scrutiny, especially thanks to the critique of anthropologists such as Boas and Montagu. While Boas emphasised the role played by environmental facts in determining alleged racial traits, Montagu compellingly questioned the very biological foundations of the concept of race.

Faced with this historical evolution, what do contemporary philosophers think about race? And how should the metaphysics of race connect with research carried out in the special sciences? As explained by Mallon (2006), there are three main camps in the philosophy of race: those who believe that races do not exist at all, and should consequently be eliminated from our discursive practices at all levels; those who believe that race is a social con-struction, perhaps based on superficial similarities, and may or may not be usefully preserved as a concept affecting social and political decisions; and, lastly, those who, directly drawing from biology, contend that races (may) exist

---

[30] Hacking emphasises that practical interests and conventional elements are so relevant for the definition of putative kinds that the notion does not play any truly useful role for us and should consequently be abandoned. For further discussion, see Cooper (2012).

in a non-essentialist sense, being determined by common ancestry and breeding, isolation, or macroscopic geographical distribution. On this latter construal, in particular, there are no truly interesting cognitive or behavioural differences emerging across racial lines – only relatively superficial differences such as skin colour and the likes; yet, actual empirical grounds exist nonetheless for preserving the concept of race (for more on this sort of racial realism, see Spencer 2018, 2018a).

From our present perspective, this case too is likely to be dealt with differently by different philosophers and does not seem to provide grounds for regarding one of the above methodological approaches as clearly more plausible than the others. In this case too, for instance, anti-naturalists – possibly taking their cue from the complexity of the indications coming from the sciences – will opt for a purely, or primarily, philosophical study of kinds, essences, properties and the likes. A moderate anti-naturalist, instead, would likely strive to find the most compelling conception of a natural kind on the basis of a priori reasoning, with a view to then using it to account for the empirical phenomena. Descriptive metaphysicians and experimental metaphysicians would focus on the concepts of kind or race as they are normally used by human subjects, correspondingly deflating the ontological question. Lastly, the more radical naturalists would bet their money on science, by either a) continuing to look at the various scientific disciplines with a view to defining the most compelling overarching account of natural kinds that can be distilled from them; or b) eliminating the metaphysical question of natural kinds altogether in favour of a philosophically oriented study of kinds as they are employed within specific scientific domains (by no means an unappealing project, at least as far as space is left for philosophy to play a genuine role, perhaps instrumental to turning purely metaphysical concepts into tools that have some use in more practical endeavours).

2.4.3 Assessment

Before closing, let us look at things form a slightly different perspective, trying to pinpoint what might be regarded as the weaknesses of each of the methodologies illustrated above.

The most radical anti-naturalists, it could be argued, make a rather questionable assumption: namely, that, in spite of the enormous success of modern and contemporary science, it is still the case that there are better ways of seeking the truth about reality, or at least formulating compelling explanations that go as deep as possible in the structure of things. In particular, notice, these anti-naturalists claim that the primacy of metaphysics and a priori reasoning holds even in the specific domains that are studied by the sciences, as it has to do with the intrinsic nature of metaphysical and scientific inquiry respectively, and not with anything like a division of labour or the kind of object under study. Upon scrutiny, it may turn out that nobody truly qualifies as an anti-naturalist in this sense nowadays. However, something like this seems to be what at least some critics of neo-Scholastic analytic metaphysics have in mind (see again Ladyman and Ross 2007 for rather explicit arguments in this sense). In relation to this, another controversial assumption that is made by at least some radical anti-naturalists, as we have seen, is that there is a peculiar form of intuition that, together with logical and conceptual analysis, allows us to gain genuine knowledge about reality largely independently of experience. In view of the almost complete lack of agreement among metaphysicians with respect to notions such as, say, fundamentality or natural kinds, one may plausibly respond, it is hard to believe that this is actually the case.

On the other hand, the role of intuition and a priori analysis might be not to unambiguously point towards the Truth but rather, as someone like Lowe would have it, to identify possible ways things could be like, and assess them on extra-empirical grounds (possibly with a view to further evaluating the remaining hypotheses with the help of science at a later stage). In this case, however, the worry arises that what appears to constitute a possible explanation of something to an historically situated subject is either dependent on or independent of contingent empirical facts involving that subject. In the former case, talk of possibility rather than Truth does not help much in arguing that metaphysics has priority over science. In the latter, instead, one is pulled back into the more radical anti-naturalist camp.[31]

As for eliminative naturalism, a potential objection to it is that it is based on the presupposition that there is nothing meaningful and interesting that can be added to scientific theories by metaphysicians. A first thought is that this flies in the face of familiar claims to the effect that there is no clear demarcation between science and non-science, hence between science and metaphysics; and that metaphysical presuppositions are always present in science both ex ante and post hoc – that is, they affect both the formulation of hypotheses and their evaluation and interpretation once they are formulated. Eliminative naturalists could respond that i) a principled distinction between science and metaphysics can in fact be drawn on the basis of clear cases – in particular, based on the possibility of performing repeatable experiments and/or on the degree of consensus and historical progress in the relevant community (which are arguably present only in science); and that ii) no matter how intermixed they are, there is simply no way to make metaphysics continuous with, and constrained by, the sciences so as to obtain metaphysical beliefs endowed with adequate epistemic credentials. More precisely, the presence of metaphysical assumptions in scientific theorising could be regarded as at

---

[31] We will say more about metaphysical possibility and alternative metaphysical explanations in the following sections.

most a temporary contingency, all respectable beliefs about the empirical domain being in fact entirely grounded in scientific methodology. Borrowing the terminology of philosophers of science, one could claim that genuinely metaphysical claims are useful only in the 'context of discovery', that is, in the phase during which scientists attempt to come up with successful explanatory hypotheses. The latter, however, gain their status based on experimental testing. Adding to this the plausible claim that whenever a hypothesis about reality can be experimentally tested it ipso facto qualifies as scientific, one obtains a biconditional that clearly rules out non-eliminative naturalism about metaphysics: an hypothesis about the world is epistemically respectable if and only if it is empirically testable, hence scientific. A relevant question remains open, however, concerning the plausibility of such a strict criterion of empirical respectability – especially after the demise of verificationist views of meaning and meaningfulness.

Considering strongly reductive naturalists next, they refrain from making the bold claim that science is an essentially autonomous and self-sufficient discipline and metaphysics should be discontinued. In some cases, they may regard this as an open possibility, and be ready to become eliminativists were it to turn out that, as a matter of fact, nothing epistemically worthy can be obtained in metaphysics in spite of the support coming from science.[32] In any event, they do acknowledge that there is (or seems to be as things currently stand) some metaphysics worth pursuing. The pressing question for them is whether the empirical input can do all the work they expect from it, as it were. Setting aside experimental metaphysics à la Goldman (which, as we have seen, replaces the ambitious goals of traditional metaphysics, that is, to uncover the fundamental structure of reality and the essential nature of things and their mutual interconnections, with the more modest task of studying our metaphysical concepts based on empirical findings), consider for instance Ladyman and Ross's views. Ladyman and Ross, as explained, have the discontinuation of neo-Scholastic metaphysics as their primary goal, and after their fierce attack against 'bad' analytic metaphysics move on straightforwardly to the recommendation of an ontology of structures. This suggests that, in Ladyman and Ross's view, there is some metaphysics more or less ready to be 'extracted' from science, in the sense that it can be inferred from the relevant scientific theories by means of relatively uncontroversial inferences, the process being almost automatic and 'only' requiring a sufficient level of knowledge of serious

---

[32] Melnyk, for instance, seems to express this attitude when he says: 'I think there is a real possibility that the activity that we call 'metaphysics' should turn out not to constitute a viable form of inquiry at all, either empirical or non-empirical' (Melnyk 2013, 81). Melnyk's essay is part of a collection of papers discussing the idea of naturalising metaphysics from various perspectives. See Ross, Ladyman and Kincaid (2013), and in particular – in addition to Melnyk's paper – the introduction and the contributions by Chakravartty (2013) and Humphreys (2013).

science, together with a bit of philosophical ingenuity and simple considerations of plausibility. However, it is far from obvious that this is the case – witness the fact that, for instance, Ladyman and Ross's own endorsement of ontic structuralism based on contemporary physics has been and still is object of intense controversy, including among seemingly respectable philosophers. While one may argue that this is because several people involved in the debate have not gained a proper understanding of the relevant scientific theories, it is also plausible to think that there is simply nothing that can be easily 'read off' of our best scientific theories in metaphysical terms.

On a similar note, experimental metaphysics in Shimony's sense certainly identifies an important dynamics, whereby science can put certain general hypotheses about reality into doubt. However, it could be objected to it that it leaves several questions open: where do the metaphysical hypotheses that we test based on science come from? What counts as a metaphysical hypothesis, exactly?[33] How does the proposed reconstruction of the testing of metaphysical hypotheses in terms of modus tollens fit with the well-known fact that there is no crucial experiment, able to conclusively falsify a given theory or conjecture rather than, say, some auxiliary hypotheses? To be sure, it is a very important fact that scientific evidence may in some cases be brought to bear on what appeared to be purely philosophical questions. What is questionable is, however, the idea that the evidential import of science can be so clear and unambiguous that it proves sufficient by itself for formulating conclusive answers to the questions at hand.

To briefly sum up, in this section we have presented the basic differentiations existing between naturalism and anti-naturalism about metaphysics and among the various formulations of each of the two. We also briefly pointed at the alleged advantages and putative shortcomings of the various positions, also on the basis of a couple of brief case studies. In the next section, we will turn to the question whether other ways of looking at the interplay between metaphysics and science can reasonably be sought.

3 What Naturalism for Metaphysics?

What was done in the final part of the previous section was by no means intended as an exhaustive assessment. It was merely aimed to provide some sense of the reasons on the basis of which philosophers have expressed doubts

---

[33] In the quantum mechanical case considered by Shimony, locality could legitimately be regarded as a very general empirical hypothesis, lacking the features that are distinctive of truly metaphysical notions – for example, the use of a sui generis vocabulary. Indeed, the assumption of locality was made by Einstein based on his theory of relativity, and he regarded it as a general presupposition for doing physics, not as a fundamental metaphysical fact or as a philosophical conjecture.

about each one of the methodologies that we have identified, be they naturalistic or anti-naturalistic in spirit. Indeed, several authors reflecting on the relationship between metaphysics and the sciences have recently attempted to find alternatives. Steering clear from both extremes (radical anti-naturalism and eliminative or strongly reductive naturalism), in particular, some have tried to find new ways of reconciling the two seemingly incompatible requests for i) continuity between science and metaphysics and ii) a sufficient degree of autonomy for metaphysics.

3.1 Vikings and Liberals

A peculiar way of attempting to achieve this goal is represented by the 'Viking approach' championed by French and McKenzie (2012, 2015). According to these two authors, those philosophers who believe that science should be a guide for the formulation of our hypotheses about reality need not, for this reason, reject or constrain traditional a priori metaphysics. This is because, as long as they are useful for the purpose, purely metaphysical concepts, categories and hypotheses can be freely employed with a view to clarifying the content of science as it evolves. That is, metaphysical tools can be instrumental to the interpretation and understanding of scientific theories quite independently of the way in which they are originally developed, and with what goals in mind. Thus, a naturalised approach to metaphysics does not require a precise, systematic methodology: to the contrary, if a particular philosopher of science finds certain elements in the metaphysical toolbox that appear handy for what they are doing, they can simply take them off the shelf and use them. French and McKenzie's favourite example is again ontic structural realism, that is, the view – endorsed, as we have seen, by Ladyman and Ross (2007) – according to which physical relations are ontologically basic. Wholeheartedly subscribing to the claim that metaphysics disengaged from the sciences is not worth pursuing per se, French and McKenzie point out at the same time that the very formulation of ontic structural realism employs concepts and theories that have been independently introduced and developed by metaphysicians – in connection for instance to dependence, truth-making, determinable and determinate properties and more. According to the Viking approach, then, in a sense non-naturalistic metaphysics – that is, metaphysics which is not continuous with, nor informed by, science – can nevertheless be of use in a naturalistic context. As a matter of fact, it should not be eliminated, as it provides philosophers interested in the sciences with instruments that would simply be unavailable to them otherwise.[34]

---

[34] This may be deemed sufficient for not classifying the Viking approach as a form of naturalism about metaphysics. Regardless of the use of labels, at any rate, what is important here is what the view says and the way in which it puts together a non-eliminative attitude towards metaphysics

Another popular position is so-called liberal naturalism (De Caro and MacArthur 2004; De Caro and Voltolini 2010; MacArthur 2019). Liberal naturalists make an ontological claim. They reject the idea that whatever entity, process or mechanism is not explicitly postulated by our best current science ipso facto qualifies as *supernatural* and, as such, should be rejected by naturalists. According to them, to the contrary, there are entities, properties, etc. that are not strictly speaking scientific yet have the right to appear in our philosophical constructions because they play an irreplaceable explanatory role. Liberal naturalists, in particular, refer to the sort of concepts that philosophers such as Sellars or Husserl emphasised the most when arguing for the irreducibility of the manifest image, the 'life world', to the scientific image: intentionality, meaning, values, normativity, and the like.

This is certainly an intriguing position, especially for those who are convinced that the sciences provide the best route to knowledge in their specific domains of application, but also believe that scientific research does not exhaust the range of meaningful activities and ways for humans to inquire into the structure of reality. On the other hand, it can be contended that liberal naturalism is an unstable position. Neta (2007), for instance, argues that there is no middle ground between 'canonical' ontological naturalism and non-naturalism. For, he says, whatever one adds to the posits of science leads immediately into the anti-naturalist camp. Indeed, that naturalists can (and should) be happy with (some) not-entirely-natural entities may sound almost like a contradiction. Importantly, however, Neta's criticism works only if one assumes that naturalism entails that metaphysics has no autonomy whatsoever – in this case, in particular, in terms of plausible requests for ontological commitment. If, instead, one defines naturalism differently – for example, as the requirement that science be regarded as an indispensable, but not exclusive, guide in formulating and assessing one's metaphysical hypotheses – then there does seem to exist room in conceptual space for something like liberal naturalism (and, more generally, for various forms of 'softer' naturalism).

3.2 Moderates

Other approaches that go along the 'softer' naturalist route rest on a primarily methodological, rather than ontological, claim. What makes them moderate rather than strongly reductive is, arguably, the willingness to accept not only the meaningfulness of metaphysical questions (thus not sharing what we called the semantic concern with metaphysics), but also the epistemic respectability of

---

and a science-first philosophical methodology. Something analogous holds for the other views of metaphysics discussed in this section.

certain answers to those questions even in cases in which these do not in any sense follow 'directly' from our best science. Moderate naturalism boils down, in a sense, to the endorsement of a less rigid attitude towards the epistemic concern with the justification of metaphysical claims.

One of these approaches is the sort of 'moderate naturalism about metaphysics' defended by Morganti and Tahko (Morganti 2013; Morganti and Tahko 2017). According to it, the correct, and most fruitful, way of conceiving the relationship between metaphysics and science is as follows. On the one hand, metaphysics is to be regarded as an autonomous enterprise aiming to explore a 'space of possibilities' – that is, possible ways things could be – based on the a priori tools of logical and conceptual analysis and model-building as well as a sui generis 'vocabulary'. Importantly, to reiterate a caveat that was already made earlier, this is not to be intended in the sense that purely a priori analysis alone may determine what is possible and what is not. Against this view, the compelling criticism can be levelled that philosophers have been wrong in the past about what is necessary and what is possible; that our thinking about modality is informed by contingent facts about our relationship with the actual world; and that one of the important things that science does is force us, every now and then, to change our most basic assumptions not only about the way things are, but also about the way they can and cannot be.[35] The idea is, rather, that, against the background of a more or less shared set of fundamental beliefs that may well be considered contingent and revisable, and certainly require updating based on the development of science, metaphysicians employ their peculiar tools with a view to gaining a deeper understanding of scientific theories and integrating them with our previous beliefs about reality, be they scientific or related to ordinary experience. And the result of this analysis is, in most cases, a number of alternative theoretical options that are best intended as possible ways things might be. On the other hand, science is primarily an inquiry into the nature of the actual world based on empirical methods. As such, it can help us pick among the options elaborated at the philosophical level, or at least provides us with precise grounds for comparatively assessing them and, at the same time, making them 'more substantial'. Indeed, the interplay between the two disciplines is conceived by Morganti and Tahko as their parallel development based on a horizontal, two-way relationship in the context of which no absolute priority claim can be made. While claiming that metaphysics makes it possible to interpret, hence fully understand, scientific

---

[35] Ladyman and Ross, for instance, rightly point out that '[p]hilosophers have often regarded as impossible states of affairs that science has [then] come to entertain' (2007, 16). They provide the examples of non-Euclidean geometry, indeterministic causation and non-absolute time. On this, see also Callender (2011).

theories, Morganti and Tahko also stress that science provides a solid basis for metaphysicians to build their theories, making their hypotheses more than mere abstract constructions.

Central to Morganti and Tahko's version of moderate naturalism is the idea that one of the main tasks of naturalistic metaphysics is one of *interpretation*. When it comes to their application for the solution of empirical and theoretical physical problems, the idea is, scientific theories are certainly autonomous and self-contained. Not so, however, when it comes to determining how exactly they describe reality, which is instead something that calls into play more general concepts and categories than those involved in the theories themselves.

Consider for instance quantum mechanics as the account of the microscopic domain that the community of physicists defined approximately between 1900 and 1935. The 'bare theory' in what has become its standard presentation of it in physics handbooks can certainly be *put to use* both in the laboratory and in the study of the theoretical physicist, and with remarkable results. However, it is unanimously regarded as requiring a lot of further work if it is to be *understood* in the proper sense of the term.[36] This means, at a first level, to eliminate the notorious 'measurement problem' arising from the fact that physical systems a) are often in 'superpositions' of several states and evolve deterministically, hence preserving superposition whenever present, yet b) are always observed to be in determinate states, without superposition, which suggests an indeterministic change of state under certain conditions.[37] At a second, more abstract level interpretation involves the assessment of the theory in relation to elements external to it – for example, the abovementioned Einsteinian assumption of locality, or entrenched beliefs about the determinateness of physical things and their properties; and the clarification of what it is about, that is, what it tells us about notions such as object, property, space and time, causality, etc. At both levels of interpretation, a substantial degree of philosophical elaboration of the theory seems in order. In fact, it appears to be irrenounceable as quantum theory is unable to provide all the required tools by itself.

Importantly, differently from more ambitious naturalists, moderate naturalists appear to think that which philosophical concepts, categories and

---

[36] Employing two abused quotes attributed to Feynman: 'If you think you understand quantum mechanics, you don't understand it', and 'Anyone who claims to understand quantum theory is either lying or crazy'.

[37] Roughly, while the theory tells us that it is typical for microscopic systems like elementary particles to be, say, here with probability 0.8 and there with probability 0.2 (a superposition of position values), when we observe one of these particles we always record a precise position (definitely here or definitely there). The same holds for all physical properties.

hypotheses and which interpretation of the relevant scientific theory should be preferred cannot be determined in anything like a straightforward way – let alone inferred directly based on the empirical and scientific input. What metaphysicians should aim for, they seem to suggest, is to be able to identify the conceptions of (a certain portion of) reality that appear admissible once both the empirical input and the results of philosophical analysis are taken into account. On that basis, one can – and ought to – then proceed to a comparative assessment of the alternatives on non-empirical grounds.[38]

Another recent approach to metaphysics that seems to fall in what we are calling the 'moderate naturalist' camp, is that presented by Emery (2023). According to Emery, most contemporary metaphysicians are naturalists about ontological commitment – in Emery's terminology, 'content naturalists'. However, since there are very good reasons for endorsing methodological naturalism if one is a content naturalist, most contemporary metaphysicians should also be methodological naturalists (or, alternatively, give up on content naturalism). On Emery's construal, methodological naturalism essentially amounts to the view that in metaphysics, as in science, we should evaluate and select our explanatory hypotheses based on empirical data plus extra-empirical considerations such as simplicity, unification and the likes. Crucially, this sets very thin constraints on acceptable metaphysical hypotheses: according to Emery, even topics that are normally regarded as paradigmatic of 'old school' metaphysics – such as, for instance, the debate about composition and the question under which conditions, if any, simpler parts constitute complex objects – may be ok for the naturalist. This, as long as the metaphysician who deals with these topics is able to provide genuine explanations, formulated

---

[38] Where this leaves us with respect to the issue of possibilities and alternative metaphysical explanations will be discussed later, as well as in the next Section. An opponent of metaphysics may follow Van Fraassen and insist that 'metaphysicians interpret what we initially understand into something hardly anyone understands' (2002, 3). However, as we have seen, the idea underlying moderate naturalism, and non-eliminative naturalism more generally, is that non-interpreted science is not as much 'understood' as 'usable', that is, it provides merely practical knowledge, which hardly deserves to be classified as a form of understanding. Moreover, once it is aptly defined and developed, metaphysics is arguably far from being incomprehensible as Van Fraassen suggests, as it systematises into appropriate categories and concepts questions that are importantly continuous with those of science on one side, and of common sense on the other. In our example, the need for a careful work of interpretation of quantum theory is hard to deny – as witnessed, among other things, by the claims made by a great physicist like Feynman, quoted a moment ago. It is interesting to notice, in this connection, that Van Fraassen himself contributed to the development of a particular interpretation of quantum mechanics (the so-called modal interpretation, see e.g., Van Fraassen 1972, 1991). Obviously enough, he has an empiricist attitude towards both quantum theory and the modal interpretation and is not interested in identifying a true ontology but only in solving the measurement problem. Again, though, the point is that it is by no means obvious that a scientific theory by itself provides all the understanding one may ask for.

on the basis of the right criteria and to engage as much as possible with the input coming from science, even if only indirectly. In the case of composition, for instance, Emery argues that a principle of 'minimal divergence' that applies both in science and in metaphysics leads us to rule out 'nihilism' – the view that, appearances notwithstanding, there are no composite objects. This is because the principle of minimal divergence invites us to prefer the hypotheses that depart the least from what appears to us to be the case, provided that they are as explanatory as the alternatives or more. Thus, in the same way in which scientists never seriously contemplate sceptical hypotheses such as, say, that elementary particles are appearances produced by an evil demon, so metaphysicians should not trade the belief that the composite objects we seem to find around us truly exist with the allegedly simpler ontology promised by a theory with mereological simples and nothing else.

In sum, on Emery's conception of naturalism, science and metaphysics have a largely shared object of study and (should) also possess a shared methodology. And it is exactly for this reason that, while it has to provide explanations that prove to be in harmony with our best science, metaphysics can preserve a significant degree of autonomy.

The idea that there is a fundamental methodological continuity between scientific and methodological inquiry is also distinctive of so-called inductive metaphysics. According to this view, metaphysics can be regarded as an a posteriori discipline, as it is based on ampliative inferences from ordinary experience and, most importantly, science.[39] At the same time, while recognising the fundamental role of science and scientific methodology, inductive metaphysics also emphasises the import of a priori methods such as conceptual analysis, as well as the need for purely philosophical notions and categories. In a sense, therefore, inductive metaphysics can be characterised as symmetrically opposite to the Canberra Plan: instead of starting from conceptual analysis and then looking at the empirical input, it works abductively from the evidence, employing conceptual analysis and other a priori tools along the way.

Another view in these surroundings is that according to which metaphysics is, like science, essentially an enterprise of model-building. Paul (2012, drawing on Godfrey-Smith 2006), for instance, argues that metaphysics is often importantly misconstrued, and the actual nature of its methodology and aims

---

[39] This approach to metaphysics is explicitly traced back to the work of rationalists such as Wolff and eighteenth-to-nineteenth-century German thinkers including Fechner, Lotze and Wundt. For more on inductive metaphysics, see the essays collected in Engelhardt et al. (2021), especially Schurz (2021). Arguably, the idea of inductive metaphysics also echoes the approach to metaphysical issues endorsed by British empiricists such as Locke and Berkeley.

misrepresented. In most (albeit not all) cases, says Paul, metaphysicians start from an initial empirical input and then try to come up with possible explanations, that is, possible theoretical models of the facts, which they evaluate and select based on abductive methods, that is, by selecting one of several available options as the most desirable on the basis of both empirical and non-empirical considerations. In this sense, once again, science and metaphysics share a common methodology, and indeed a common origin: that is, the human inclination towards general, encompassing accounts of the phenomena. These, says Paul, have the form of models, whose ability to explain and provide understanding is determined by the capacity that human inquirers possess to proceed abductively beyond the empirical facts.

3.3 Overview and Discussion

As in the previous section, we will now look at sample metaphysical issues which, besides exhibiting a significant interplay between metaphysics and science, also point at some problems and open questions – in particular for the theoretical and methodological views introduced in the present section. Two case studies will be briefly considered: the first concerns free will, the second ontic indeterminacy and quantum mechanics.

3.3.1 The Problem of Free Will and the Sciences

Let us say that an agent (not necessarily a human agent) has free will if they are ultimately responsible for their actions. That is, they are in the strict sense the authors of those actions, hence responsible for them and the events they cause. Philosophical analysis has led to distinguish, first of all, between freedom of will and freedom of action: it looks as though one may be unable, for reasons independent of them, to act as they intend to, or to act differently from the way the act, yet still be free to decide one way rather than another. It is essentially this latter sort of autonomy – involving our decisions and not (just) our actions – that is the object of discussion among philosophers.

   A key question is whether free will in this sense is compatible with determinism. Determinism is the thesis that the state of the universe at a given time together with the laws of nature determine uniquely the state of the universe at the immediately later time. More generally, the future is entirely determined by what happened in the past. If determinism is true, then it looks as though there is no free will, as someone's decisions – however closely linked with what they recognise as *their* reasons – are not up to them, and instead depend entirely on the state of the universe and the laws of nature. Now, the truth or falsity of determinism seems best regarded as a contingent matter, to be decided based on observation and scientific knowledge. Prima facie, it seems plausible to think that at the macroscopic level at which human actions take place, the relevant events (be they neurophysiological, biological, or physical) are governed by deterministic laws. This has led some philosophers to define a 'compatibilist' view according to which determinism and free will can peacefully coexist, at least provided that the latter is understood as freedom to act. That is, in the sense that a person is free if they make their decisions without any form of coercion (additional to that of the laws of nature) and based on reasons that they (would normally) recognise as their own. In this sense, compatibilism rejects the idea that responsibility and freedom require that one be, so to put it, the cause of the universe going in one direction rather than another, equally realisable one. In fact, this latter scenario is ruled out at the outset, hence the original, stronger sense of freedom of the will is simply unavailable. On the other side, as could be expected, one finds the 'incompatibilists', who believe that there simply is no free will if determinism is true. One important reason for thinking so is the 'Consequence Argument' (Ginet 1966; Van Inwagen 1983), which purports to show that if determinism is true then nothing is, and has ever been, really up to any agent, as everything is fixed given the universe at the Big Bang and the laws of nature. 'Hard incompatibilists' conclude from this that there is no free will in the actual world, while 'libertarians' insist that there is free will in the stronger sense, hence determinism is false.

To support this latter claim, physics is often called into play. Quantum theory, some say, is an indeterministic theory, and it is the currently accepted theory of the microscopic world. Therefore, one may contend that the processes in people's brain leading to their decisions and ensuing actions are essentially indeterministic, as they are ultimately grounded in microscopic facts and events. This would mean that the previous history of the universe is in fact compatible with an agent acting in more than one way, hence that free will in the stronger sense of the term (as freedom to will, not just to act) is possible, and may even be actual, after all. This, however, is far from straightforward, and several questions at the boundary between philosophy and science arise. A first important thing to point out is that quantum mechanics is in fact a family of theories/interpretations, and generic talk of quantum indeterminism is unlikely to lead to any progress in the attempt to clarify the issues concerning human deliberation and action. The issue of providing an explication of the theory – in particular, with a view to solving the measurement problem – should no doubt be dealt with first. This may even lead, notice, to an entirely deterministic theoretical framework, as in Bohmian mechanics and many-worlds interpretations. Setting this aside for the time being, at any rate, one may legitimately worry that quantum indeterminism leads to the idea that we are not truly free anyway, as it is just a matter of chance or 'luck' whether our decisions will lead to one course of action or the other.[40] Also, isn't microscopic indeterminism in any case irrelevant at the macroscopic domain where human agents are located?

A compelling model of free action should, first of all, be provided based on quantum indeterminism. An important effort in this sense has already been made, in particular by Robert Kane. In several writings (starting from Kane 1996), Kane argued that, at least for a proper subset of our decisions, it can be the case that the outcome of one's deliberation is the result of an indeterministic process and, at the same time, the agent is strictly the author of the decision, the one responsible for its consequences, etc. This is because the indeterministic processes in question begin with a state of superposition between distinct options that have been selected (also) in virtue of the subject's reasons, desires, motivations, etc.; and since the process of deliberation is entirely internal to the subject, regardless of what the final outcome turns out to be the it can be regarded as entirely due to an effort made by the agent.

Still, one may wonder, does the fact that the relevant quantum processes are internal to the subject truly suffice for making justice to our intuition that the subject must be responsible for their decisions? After all, on the proposed construal, which process, and with what outcome, will determine (or, maybe better, constitute) the agent's deliberation and ensuing action is still entirely random. On this note, a better differentiation may be in order between *indeterminism* and *indeterminacy*. Perhaps what is truly relevant is not the former, that is, that given the laws of nature there is a degree of chance in the jump from one state to the next; but rather the latter, that is, that given the nature of the relevant physical systems more than two 'options' (i.e., superposed states) exist.[41] Indeed, as we have just seen, scientifically minded supporters of free will have often depicted decisions as analogous to indeterministic, hence chancy, measurement processes. What if the right analogy were instead with the 'reaction' of a physical system to being measured, that is, with the fact that – very loosely speaking! – a particle in an indeterminate state 'picks' its preferred outcome among the possible ones?[42] And what if such picking could be

---

[40] For, indeterminism amounts to there being more than one possible evolution from an initial state, which one becomes actual being entirely random. If so, one would be 'lucky' in case their decisions led them to the 'right' course of action, as indeterminism entails that in exactly the same situation, both externally and internally, the subject could have chosen in the exactly opposite, hence 'wrong', way. This is the well-known 'luck argument' (see, e.g., Haji 1999).

[41] What quantum indeterminacy amounts to, as we will see in the next case study, is itself open to discussion.

[42] In connection to this, the further idea could be explored that the selection of the possible alternatives may well involve the agent's reasons, whereas the decision itself might boil down to mere 'picking' in the sense of Ullmann-Margalit and Morgenbesser (1977).

conceived of as the determinate starting point of an entirely deterministic sequence of events? One may venture as far as to claim that the postulation of a form of 'event causation', or even 'agent causation', is not necessarily in tension with proper naturalistic methodology as is often thought.[43]

Be this as it may, moving to the issue of the (ir)relevance of microscopic indeterminacy for free will two more sources of scientific input are relevant. First: while, as mentioned earlier, it is normally taken for granted that ours is an essentially deterministic world, it is in fact not so obvious that the domain in which agents make choices and act is deterministic. To the contrary, it can be argued that it is very much an open question how the relevant physics relates to the relevant biology and neurophysiology (see Balaguer 2010; Roskies 2014; Ellis 2016). Second: there are by now a host of experimental results that allegedly show that free will is an illusion. These results have been the object of intense discussion for more than 20 years now, starting from Libet's (Libet 2002) famous claim that there is activity in our brain way before our conscious decisions, strongly suggesting that our choices and actions are predetermined (see also Wegner 2002). The actual significance of Libet-type results and claims has been convincingly questioned[44], but there is definitely room for further work here as well.

What should metaphysicians learn from the foregoing (if anything)? Unlike what we did in the previous section, we will not discuss this case study (nor the following one) in connection to each one of the views on methodology that we have illustrated. Instead, we will make a few general considerations, and say a bit more about a specific one of the approaches presented in this section. The general remarks have to do with the fact that the issue of free will appears paradigmatic in the following two senses: a) there is a wealth of scientific facts and open areas of empirical research that are directly relevant to the philosophical issue at hand; b) nothing like a clear-cut answer to the initial question can be expected to come (currently, at least) from science. Fact b) might invite die-hard anti-naturalists to insist that a solution to the problem should be sought through the methods of traditional a priori metaphysics. Fact a), on the other hand, pulls in the opposite direction. Intermediate, moderate forms of naturalism might thus

---

[43] These are two forms of 'top-down' causation, that is, causation going from more complex to less complex entities, which are often invoked by libertarians to express the sui generis powers of human (perhaps, more generally, living) agents. In the former case, the focus is on higher-level properties and the events they determine; in the latter, on agents as sui generis substances. Both views, and in particular agent causation, are normally looked at with suspicion by naturalists – possibly because of some underlying physicalists/reductionist assumptions (see the earlier discussion of physicalism).

[44] See, for instance, Nahmias (2014), and Schurger et al. (2021).

appear an ideal solution, at least in cases like this. However, these too have problems to face.

Consider, for instance, liberal naturalism. As we have seen, liberal naturalists allow for non-scientific entities in their ontology as long as i) they do not contradict science and ii) they play an explanatory role with respect to some relevant facts. To be sure, this entails the need for independent, non-question-begging criteria for distinguishing the 'good' from the 'bad' in the set of 'supernatural' entities. In other words, if the only constraints on acceptable metaphysical hypotheses are i) and ii) above, then the worry might surface that really little – if anything – can be coherently left out while still remaining in the naturalist camp. Hudson (2016), for instance, argues that even the hypothesis of a creating God is not necessarily in conflict with current science, and can indeed add to its explanatory power – in particular, by telling a story that goes beyond the point where the Big Bang reconstruction necessarily stops. Hudson, however, explicitly presents his views as non-naturalistic. What exactly is it – if anything – that demarcates this from a sufficiently liberalised naturalism? Liberal naturalists could respond that the naturalistically inadmissible ontological posits are those that – although they do not literally contradict scientific theories – provide explanations that conflict with the spirit of the scientific method. In Hudson's scenario, conjecturing a God that makes it so that the Big Bang takes place is compatible with the Big Bang story by construction, yet adds to the latter something that is in principle not testable, and radically unlike the sort entities, mechanisms and processes normally hypothesised by physicists. One may object to this line of argument, though, that it is unclear why the same should not apply to many (if not all) the things that liberal naturalists are happy to include in their ontology, such as intentionality and normativity.[45]

What should one think specifically about free will? Is it relevant enough in our 'Lebenswelt' to be postulated independently of science (perhaps with vague concessions to the effect that we should be ready to give it up were science to conclusively (?) show that it does not exist)? And if we do assume realism about free will, how exactly should we conceive of it in the light of the contrasting indications coming from the empirical domain with respect to determinism, indeterminism, etc.? Is event/agent causation incompatible with naturalistic

---

[45] Physicalism intended as the view that everything is ultimately analysable in terms of a future physics may solve the problem for the liberal naturalist. For, one may argue, physics will provide the tools for analysing and possibly reducing normativity and free will, but most likely not God. However, as we have already seen, talk of an ideal future physics threatens to make physicalism empty. In particular, it remains unclear why exactly we should deem certain things non-physical in principle based merely on current physics (together perhaps with some entrenched common sense beliefs).

methodology, or space exists for the naturalist to coherently revise the idea that physics is 'causally closed', that is, fundamental physical properties do all the causal work involved in bringing about effects in the physical world?[46] Should, perhaps, the default position not be one of ontological commitment, but rather neutrality and agnosticism? On all these questions, the liberal naturalist methodology does not seem to provide clear indications – on the other hand, whether and to what extent other approaches fare better is yet to be seen.

3.3.2 Ontic Indeterminacy and Quantum Mechanics

We have mentioned quantum indeterminacy in the previous sub-section. Our second example concerns precisely the notions of vagueness and indeterminacy, in direct connection with quantum physics.[47] It is quite uncontroversial that some concepts, such as those expressed by predicates like 'bald' or 'heap', are intrinsically imprecise in the sense that it is vague where the boundary is which separates cases in which those concepts apply and cases in which they do not. It is an interesting question, however, whether in addition to the epistemic indeterminacy related to linguistic/conceptual vagueness, and possibly as the cause of the latter in at least some cases, one may also find lack of determinateness in the world itself.

When indeterminacy is taken to be a feature of things rather than concepts, it seems to involve *identity*. On this construal, an object a is said to be indeterminate if there is some b such that it is indeterminate whether a is b. Evans (1978) famously provided a (putative) impossibility proof for ontic indeterminacy so intended: granting that it is indeterminate whether a is b, he argued, one gets that there is a determinate difference between the properties of a and those of b: b is such that it is indeterminate whether a is identical to it, while a is not.[48] From this, it follows – via Leibniz's Law[49] – that a and b are determinately distinct, hence a is not an ontically indeterminate object after all. There is general agreement nowadays that Evans falls short of showing that the notion of

---

[46] Here, notice, the problem of providing a precise definition of 'physical' emerges again. Depending on whether one identifies fundamental physical properties with those designated as such by current theories or, instead, with properties that will be part of a future physics, one's take on the issue of causal closure might change significantly.

[47] For a much more detailed treatment, see the Element recently authored by Torza (2023).

[48] More specifically, turning *de dicto* predication into *de re* predication, it can be shown that b has the property that it is indeterminate whether a is it. But, by the necessity of self-identity, that is, the logical truth of $a=a$, a has the property that it is determinate that a is it (i.e., itself), which obviously entails that a does not have the property that it is indeterminate whether a is it.

[49] Also known as the Principle of the Indiscernibility of the Identicals, it says that if a is identical to b, then a and b have the same properties.

ontically indeterminate identity is intrinsically contradictory.[50] And here is where science comes in.

As first noticed by Lowe (1994), a relatively simple way to refute Evans' argument is by pointing out that quantum theory is best understood in terms of ontic indeterminacy (which is something we have already seen). Lowe considers the case of an atom absorbing an electron at a given time, and then emitting an electron at a later time. Since the absorbed electron typically comes to coexist with one or more exactly similar particles orbiting at a given distance from the atom's nucleus, and the theory gives us no reason for identifying the emitted electron with any one of these particles rather than another, Lowe concludes that it is ontically indeterminate whether the emitted electron is the same as the absorbed electron and, more generally, that the identity of quantum particles is (or at least may be) indeterminate. Later authors, such as French and Krause (1995) mounted a seemingly stronger case focusing on exactly similar quantum particles in the same state, that is, on situations such as that considered by Lowe, but independently of diachronic considerations. One remarkable fact about these objects, French and Krause point out, is that they seem to violate the Principle of the Identity of the Indiscernibles, as they have all the same properties (in the form of objective probability assignments) including location.[51] Also, they display a statistical behaviour which is insensitive to which particle is which. Essentially, while in the macroscopic domain the possible states available to a number of objects can be determined based on intuitive combinatorial calculations, this is not the case in the quantum domain. In particular, exchanging the particles does not make any physical difference, and it can consequently be conjectured that particles lack determinate identities – the impossibility of identifying specific particles consequently being due to more than purely epistemic limitations.

More recently, quantum indeterminacy has been explored further in the form of indeterminacy concerning the *properties* of quantum systems rather than (or

---

[50] The basic point is that Evans makes certain assumptions that, intuitive as they may seem, cannot be considered innocent when it comes to identity and to establishing whether it is determinate or indeterminate. For instance, that we can refer specifically, that is, determinately, to *a* or to *b* while attempting to establish whether their identities are (in)determinate. There is also agreement, however, that resisting Evans' argument is not straightforward and requires one to make non-trivial choices at the level of logic and/or metaphysics.

[51] This is the converse of Leibniz's Law above. That quantum particles (can) violate the Identity of the Indiscernibles is, however, controversial. Although it has been taken for granted for a certain period, such a claim has recently lost popularity in favour of the idea that quantum objects are always at least weakly discernible, that is, they obey a version of the Identity of the Indiscernibles that ranges over symmetric, irreflexive relations. Others even say that, under sensible assumptions about the theory, particles are in fact always discernible in the traditional sense. At any rate, this is not crucial for our present discussion. For more details, see French (2019) and Bigaj (2022).

in addition to) their identity conditions. The relevant fact is that one of the distinctive features of the theory is, as we have seen, that it allows for states of superposition. That is, states in which a system is attributed a non-zero probability for more than one value for a certain physical quantity (in fact, for certain sets of physical quantities). Modulo some very plausible assumptions about the theory and its interpretation,[52] this leads straightforwardly to an explanation in terms of property indeterminacy. Typical quantum systems, that is to say, can be in a state whereby it is indeterminate which value for a certain property they exemplify – or, slightly differently, in a state in which they exemplify an indeterminate value for that property. Granting this view of the quantum domain, however, it is then an open question how best to understand the nature of quantum properties and quantum indeterminacy more generally (on this, see Calosi and Mariani 2021).[53]

The significance of this case study is, thus, analogous to that of the previous one (and of those we considered earlier in this Element). Besides providing at least some reasons for endorsing naturalism about metaphysics, it confirms that even in the context a scientifically informed metaphysics finding clear answers and identifying the most plausible explanations and hypotheses is by no means an easy task. In this sense, the reflection on ontic indeterminacy may be regarded as a paradigmatic example of moderately naturalistic metaphysics: autonomous reflection by analytic metaphysicians (as well as logicians and philosophers of language) turns out to be useful for understanding certain scientific hypotheses; in turn, the latter provide a firm basis for applying such reflection to the actual world, as well as for comparatively assessing the various alternatives one finds at the level of mere metaphysical possibility. In connection to this, importantly, ontic indeterminacy is in no way entailed by quantum theory. Rather, it is a notion that may be usefully employed for understanding certain aspects of the theory. At the same time, quantum mechanics appears to put constraints on admissible general theories of ontic indeterminacy, but nothing more. Thus, several important questions remain open: should we be 'conservative 'and stick to the idea that indeterminacy is always an epistemic matter, consequently opting for other interpretations of the evidence – if not for antirealism about quantum mechanics? Or is, to the contrary, ontic indetermin-

---

[52] In particular, that quantum probabilities are objective and do not just express partial knowledge; and that there is a direct correspondence between probability values and actual physical properties.

[53] Some theories of ontic indeterminacy, for instance, seem to have problems in taking into account the contextuality of quantum properties, that is, the seeming dependence of their values, at least in some cases, on how they are measured (see Held 2022, especially section 5.3). For an overview of different accounts of ontic indeterminacy, see again Torza (2023).

acy the best way of making sense of what an undoubtedly successful theory tells us about the world? If it is, how exactly should it be understood and analysed? Under what assumptions – linguistic, metaphysical and at the level of the interpretation of physical theory – does ontic indeterminacy make the most sense? As for quantum systems, are they truly indeterminate at the object level? Does their alleged indeterminacy concern identities or properties (or both)?

3.3.3 Assessment

Milder, intermediate formulations of naturalism about metaphysics may be considered appealing in that they do not question the autonomy of metaphysics, but at the same time fully endorse the idea that it should be as continuous as possible with science. At the same time, several points need to be clarified concerning how the proposed methodologies should exactly be expected to translate in practice.

As we have seen, for instance, liberal naturalists claim that there is a non-empty set of supernatural yet scientifically acceptable entities. However, pending the specification of criteria on the basis of which to fill the set, as it were, the risk exists that this is uninformative (and, possibly, that ontological commitment ends up being defined largely independently of science).

As for supporters of the Viking approach, they are explicit that they put forward nothing more than an opportunistic, pragmatic and non-systematic perspective whereby metaphysics should be appropriated by philosophers of science whenever and in whatever way they find it useful. But exactly for this reason, the approach falls short of providing specific guidelines and criteria for the evaluation of competing hypotheses and explanations.

What about what we labelled here 'moderate naturalism' (i.e., the family of views according to which metaphysics and science naturally complement each other in connection to at least some questions about the nature of things, and perhaps share a common methodology based on abductive reasoning and model-building, yet metaphysics should preserve its autonomy even in a naturalistic setting)? If metaphysics should be informed, but is not entailed, by scientific theories, and there typically are several possible metaphysical frameworks that are equally compatible with the relevant science, then it is crucial to know how to choose among competing options, and what role non-empirical considerations ought to play in this connection. Unfortunately, this has historically proven to be a very complex issue. To be clear, the problem is not limited to moderate naturalism à la Morganti and Tahko or Emery. To the contrary, it affects all those contexts, including scientific ones, in which the available data are equally compatible with several, mutually conflicting explanatory hypotheses. Arguably, the avoidance of this very problem is an important reason for the popularity of some of the methodologies that we have discussed earlier: in particular, eliminativist approaches (no metaphysics, no problem of choosing one particular metaphysics over another), radical anti-naturalism (conceptual analysis, the recourse to common sense and ordinary language and rational intuition are likely to lead us directly to the Truth, not just to under-determined possibilities) and strongly reductive naturalism (metaphysics can be read off directly from science, hence the problem of theory-choice is only relevant in the scientific domain – where, however, it is not particularly worrying in practice, as it is a fact that the scientific community chooses routinely one theory over others).

A confirmation of the centrality of this issue of theory assessment and hypothesis selection comes from the case studies that we have considered here, and indeed from those presented in the rest of this Element too. In each one of them it appeared clear that, significant as empirical evidence and scientific theorising may be, science falls short of providing sufficient input for giving a final answer to the initial questions. And, lest metaphysicians be attributed once again some special form of intuition or other capacity to discover the Truth, bringing philosophical tools to bear on the matter is not enough either. Consider, for instance, free will: welcome as the interaction between science and metaphysics is when it comes to shedding light on such an important philosophical topic, it is far from providing unambiguous results. At the same time, metaphysical analysis can identify different theoretical alternatives with rigour and precision, but several – more or less equally respectable – views on freedom of will and actionfreedom of will and action systematically remain available nonetheless. Things are rendered even more complicated by the relevance of further factors – most notably, in this latter case, the significance of free will for our very perception of ourselves and what is distinctive of us. A similar dynamics can be traced, for instance, in the case study, considered in the previous section, concerning natural kinds. There too, scientific progress has made it possible to turn a purely philosophical question into one that can be dealt with also on the basis of the empirical evidence. However, as things stand, it seems implausible to think that anything conclusive can be said about whether natural kinds exist and, if so, what they are. Depending on the specific domain, one will at most find good reasons for making certain restricted claims (e.g., that natural kinds exist at the level of elementary particles); for suspending one's judgment (claiming, e.g., that it is advisable not to take the existence of well-defined psychiatric disorders for granted); or, alternatively, for stating clearly that one's opinion are crucially grounded on something more than relatively uncontroversial empirical facts (as, e.g., in the case of race, where several philosophers openly acknowledge that the basis for their views is mostly if not exclusively of a pragmatic nature). In all these cases, once again the position one decides to take with respect to the issues at hand may ultimately be grounded in acceptance rather than belief, that is, in the endorsement of a stance rather than in explicit argument.[54]

In conclusion, then, even assuming that there are good reasons for abandoning extreme anti-naturalistic and radical naturalistic views, and instead facing the big philosophical questions (whenever possible) with both the tools of metaphysics and those of science along the lines of milder forms of naturalism, the issue remains concerning whether a clear, shared methodology is available – or at least can be defined – for evaluating our metaphysical hypotheses and selecting among them. In the next section, we will try to say a bit more about this.

4 Metaphysics, Science and Theory Choice

In the previous section, we stressed the fact that it is very difficult to identify precise strategies for comparatively assessing our metaphysical constructions, regardless of how much into contact with the best available scientific theories one puts them. Indeed, unless one believes that something like rational intuition guides us directly to the Truth, all we have to work with is logical consistency and vague requests for compatibility with science. In more detail, if scientific theories do not strictly speaking entail metaphysical conclusions, and there are always several alternative metaphysical hypotheses for the explanation of a given fact or set of facts, then the problem is essentially a familiar one: that is, a problem of under-determination. As a matter of fact, albeit to a different degree given their nature and aims, both science and metaphysics are under-determined by the empirical data. This justifies the claim that – in metaphysics as in science – ampliative reasoning plays a central role and certain theoretical virtues[55] must be taken into account when evaluating one's hypotheses and proposed explanations. In this final section, we examine these notions in more detail, comparing the dynamics of theory choice and the role of theoretical virtues in science and in metaphysics, and attempting on this basis a more general assessment of the prospects for a 'scientifically respectable' metaphysics.

---

[54] The reader is referred again to Chakravartty (2017). Interestingly in view of our discussion in this section, Chakravartty explicitly connects the idea of a stance to that of explanatory power, suggesting that different epistemic stances will put different weights on i) how much a certain metaphysical hypothesis or posit is empirically supported and on ii) how much it explains.

[55] I will use 'non-empirical' and 'theoretical' interchangeably in what follows.

4.1 Theoretical Virtues in Science and Metaphysics

So-called theoretical or 'non-empirical' virtues include things like simplicity, coherence with other beliefs, fruitfulness, non-ad-hocness and more, which may be plausibly considered relevant when evaluating a putative explanation E of certain facts, in particular when alternative accounts E', E", ... of the same facts exist that are equally compatible with such facts but also inconsistent with E. The reason for the terminology should appear obvious: two theories that both account for the phenomena in a given domain can clearly be comparatively assessed only with respect *to the way in which* they do so, that is, with respect to non-empirical factors concerning the theories themselves. Indeed, whether one of the competing theories is, say, simpler than the other in some sense is a non-empirical issue, since it has to do with the linguistic structure of the two theories broadly understood and not with the empirical domain that structure is about – which is the same by assumption. Something similar holds for coherence, unifying power and the other virtues in the same group.

Now, theoretical virtues have been much discussed in the philosophy of science especially since the seminal work of Kuhn.[56] The common wisdom is that there is no unique way to systematically put together all these non-empirical elements so as to provide an objective basis for preferring one theoretical framework over another. As a result, theoretical virtues are often regarded as playing at best a pragmatic role, providing some guidance in theory choice in particular cases, but nothing like a rigorous framework or even an algorithm.[57] In view of this fact and, more generally, of their essential nature, theoretical virtues have also been widely considered not to be truth-conducive – that is, such that the fact that a theory T possesses one or more of them to a high degree is not an indicator that T is true or approximately true. Indeed, on the one hand, if there is no unique, objective way of putting all of them together and provide a precise evaluation of a given theory in terms of its 'virtuosity', how could one claim that virtuous theories are (approximately) true or likely to be (approximately) true? The same holds, of course, if there is no unique, objective way of quantifying individual virtues. Consider again simplicity: if E is simpler than E' in some respect/from the perspective of one subject but not in some other respect/from the perspective on another subject, on what basis would one claim that E is more likely to be true than E' (or vice versa)? What is more, for any non-empirical virtue or combination of non-empirical virtues one looks at, the fact that a proposed hypothesis, theory or explanation unquestionably

---

[56] See in particular Kuhn (1977). Also Thagard (1978) and, for a recent treatment, Schindler (2018).

[57] For interesting discussions, see Okasha (2011) and Stegenga (2015).

exemplifies it to a high degree is entirely compatible with the world being very different from what the theory describes.

As far as science is concerned, the problem of the role of extra-empirical virtues in theory choice is at least partly constrained by objective matters of fact. First of all, as mentioned, one can point out that there are certain theories that scientists, for whatever reason, end up preferring. Consequently, an assessment of theoretical virtues may be regarded as primarily – if not exclusively – relevant for the post hoc philosophical evaluation of the specific theories that were selected by the scientific community based on a clear consensus. Also, the difficult question whether extra-empirical virtues are truth-conducive is not particularly pressing in the case of science. For, an empiricist/instrumentalist approach to scientific theories and hypotheses is perfectly viable and, more generally, a reference to the notion of truth is not essential to the definition of science, nor to the implementation of the scientific method, empirical adequacy arguably being the primary aim for scientists.[58]

In the case of metaphysics, instead, one cannot find a clear consensus on any particular issue, nor any obvious form of empirical success. While not being a bad thing per se, this certainly urges philosophers to at least seek some criteria for making reasoned choices among alternative hypotheses. Moreover, since metaphysics is normally characterised as being i) in the business of seeking the truth about reality as well as ii) significantly detached from the empirical input, the question concerning the truth-conduciveness of extra-empirical virtues appears inescapable in the case of metaphysical hypotheses.[59]

It is not surprising, then, that some authors have put forward rather sceptical claims about the status of metaphysical inquiry. On the one hand, the worry has been expressed that the nature of under-determination, hence the strength of explanation, is crucially different in science and in metaphysics. Ladyman (2012), for instance, makes a claim to this effect, pointing out that theoretical virtues cannot be expected to play the same role they play in the scientific context when it comes to theories that – like those of a priori metaphysics – lack

---

[58] Which is not to say that the debate between scientific realists and antirealists, concerning the epistemic value of scientific theories, is not meaningful – far from it. Interestingly, though, non-empirical virtues do not play a central role in that debate, the main focus being, instead, on what the most compelling explanation of the success of science could be and whether the right amount of historical continuity can be found across theory change. See, however, Schindler (2018) for the view that a careful consideration of non-empirical virtues – in particular, simplicity, fertility and non ad-hocness – can be instrumental to the development of a compelling realist attitude towards science.

[59] To make just one example, Lewis famously stated that '[t]he benefits [of modal realism] are worth their ontological cost. Modal realism is *fruitful*; that gives us good reason to believe that it is *true*' (1986, 4, emphasis added).

a proper connection with the empirical data.[60] Similarly, Saatsi (2017) argues that, even assuming that 'explanationism'[61] is truth-conducive in science, abductive assessments of rival metaphysical hypotheses are much more doubtful. Lastly, Bueno and Shalkowski (2020) argue that the history of science does not lend clear support to the claim that the scientific community routinely selects among alternative explanations based on theoretical virtues; and that doing so is, in any case, a non-starter in metaphysics, as it basically boils down to simply assuming the truth of the explanation at hand. If correct, these claims clearly put important limitations to the degree of autonomy of metaphysics in a naturalistic context, and seemingly urge a strongly reductive, if not altogether eliminative, attitude towards the metaphysical enterprise. Where metaphysicians, in particular those of the naturalistic camp, can go from here is thus a pressing open question.

4.2 Open Questions and Avenues for Further Research

Two main routes seem available for those metaphysicians who are willing to undertake the task of defining a more precise view of metaphysical theory assessment. First, a more careful analysis of theoretical virtues in the scientific and metaphysical domain, and of the forms of reasoning that are employed in the process of defining and updating our beliefs and hypotheses about reality. Secondly, further reflection on the very nature and aims of metaphysics, especially in its naturalistic varieties, in light of the problems just pointed out.

Let us start from the first option. To begin with, the broadly Kuhnian view that no organic treatment of theoretical virtues is possible is by no means unassailable. For one, the strongest results against the possibility of a systematic treatment of theoretical virtues – such as, for instance, those in Okasha (2011) – assume a 'no dictatorship' condition, to the effect that no virtue ever overrides all the others, not even empirical adequacy. This assumption could be disputed. One way of doing this could be by looking at the opinions of practising researchers. Schindler (2022), for instance, based on a survey on theoretical virtues in science involving natural and social scientists as well as philosophers, found a rather significant agreement on a particular ranking (internal consistency>accuracy>predictive power>unification>external consistency>simplicity). Other attempts at systematisation have been made, on a less

---

[60] Schurz (2021) claims that metaphysical hypotheses can be abductively justified on the basis of two important criteria often regarded as distinctive of good scientific hypotheses: unification and independent testability. This, however, is a minority view whose generalisability to metaphysics as a whole is yet to be assessed – and currently appears doubtful.

[61] That is, the methodology of using inference to the best explanation in theory choice, and making theoretical virtues count in determining what qualifies as best.

experimental basis, by Douglas (2013), Mackonis (2013), McMullin (2014) and Keas (2018).

Nothing of this sort exists in metaphysics, however – nor, a fortiori, in relation to the choice of different ways of putting metaphysical and scientific hypotheses together.[62] Further work on theoretical virtues in metaphysics, then, is both possible and advisable. And it would certainly be interesting to examine these issues from both a theoretical and an empirical viewpoint – examining, for instance, how belief updating and the ranking of virtues works in the actual practice of metaphysicians.

In this connection, some theoretical virtues may turn out to play a different role in science and in metaphysics. For instance, on at least some possible conceptions of naturalism about metaphysics the stated aim is to provide an overarching view of the world: one that makes use of the general concepts and categories of metaphysics but is at the same time rendered credible by its being based on the best available science. In view of the inevitable dialectics between the manifest image and the scientific image of the world, ideally such a construction should additionally be capable of accounting for our common sense perception of reality – if only by providing an explanation of the reason why, and extent to which, it is wrong or misleading. Now, a crucial aspect of this dynamics is that it involves independent sets of beliefs. Consequently, a virtue that is probably not so important in science is likely to play instead a crucial role in metaphysical theory choice: *external consistency*. In seeking a unified, consistent belief set in this context, moreover, particular choices have to be made among conflicting beliefs belonging to distinct belief systems (science, philosophy, common sense). Depending on whether one gives priority, say, to the (allegedly) revisionary indications coming from the sciences or to our established common sense beliefs, clearly one's current belief system will be updated in potentially radically differ-ent directions. In relation to this, another non-empirical virtue which is often underestimated and equally often misunderstood may plausibly be taken to play a fundamental role in the case of metaphysical theory choice: that is, the *conser-vation of established beliefs* (see Morganti 2013 and Emery 2023). That is, the

---

[62] Simplicity/parsimony has been considered in some detail, in isolation from the other virtues by Nolan (1997), Sober (2009, 2015, 2022), Cowling (2013), Brenner (2017), Jansson and Tallant (2017) and Norton (2021). Morganti (2013) examines some case-studies from physics and emphasises the importance of the virtue of conservativeness, that is, of the minimisation in the change of established beliefs in view of novel input from science (more on this in a moment), but no more systematic claim is made. Emery (2023), as we have seen, convincingly endorses that the same extra-empirical factors guide theory-choice in science and in metaphysics, but admits that hers is a starting project and limits herself to the careful illustration of three examples (concerning laws of nature, composition and presentism and actualism in connection to the theory of relativity). Mohammadian (2017) attempts a parallel, exhaustive examination of theoretical virtues in science and metaphysics, but does not reach any overarching conclusion.

idea that in evaluating competing hypotheses we value the minimisation of the subsequent changes in our established belief system. The pragmatist William James, for one, notoriously claimed that when updating 'his previous mass of opinions [...one...] saves as much as he can, for in this matter of belief we are all extreme conservatives. So he tries to change first this opinion, and then that [...], until at last some new idea comes up which he can graft upon the ancient stock with a minimum of disturbance of the latter' (1907/79, lecture II, 'What Pragmatism Means'). An analogous idea was developed by Quine in terms of 'minimum mutilation' of one's established beliefs (Quine and Ullian 1978). To avoid potential ambiguities, the idea of being conservative and minimising revision does *not* contradict the undeniable fact that science has often led us to radically change our ways of conceiving of reality, and that regardless of what happens during those that Kuhn would call periods of 'normal science', what is truly distinctive of the sciences is their ability and tendency to give rise to deep conceptual revolutions. There is no such contradiction here because what the virtue of conservatism invites one to do is to i) integrate the results of science – which, at least on a naturalistic perspective, are never put into doubt – into a larger context in which beliefs of a different origin are also present; and then ii) evaluate alternative ways of eliminating any inconsistency that may arise by modifying our initial beliefs as little as possible, always bearing in mind that simply ignoring scientific 'facts' is not an option (at least not for naturalists). Therefore, the sense of conservativeness at stake here does not boil down to the (implausible) rejection of scientific beliefs that conflict with our entrenched ways of seeing the world. Rather, as clearly expressed in the above quotation from James, the criterion at stake recommends that the interpretation of the relevant scientific theories (which, recall, is never obvious given a theory on its own) and the evaluation of the possibilities that are individuated by the a priori work of the metaphysicians are carried out in such a way that an ideal balance is found between novelty and preservation. As Emery puts it, one should endorse the principle of minimal divergence, according to which 'Insofar as you have two or more candidate theories, all of which are empirically and explanatory adequate, you ought to choose the theory that diverges least from the manifest image' (2023; 131). Indeed, so understood, the virtue of conservativeness is by no means a guiding criterion in metaphysics only – let alone in 'bad', unscientific metaphysics only. As suggested by James and Quine and Ullian, and explicitly stated by Emery, the need to 'minimise divergence' is ubiquitous, and intrinsic to the basic workings of the human intellect – or so it can be argued.

This leads us to another important area for further inquiry, which concerns the specific forms of reasoning that guide theory choice. A careful consideration of inference to the best explanation/abductive reasoning (the two are not exactly synonyms but can harmlessly be identified for present purposes) would certainly be a useful starting point for those wishing to make the dynamics of theory choice clearer and their philosophical analysis more rigorous. For, surely, it is the sort of reasoning that guides us whenever the alternatives are empirically under-determined.[63] A relevant question in this context is whether the ampliative sort of reasoning under discussion can be analysed in probabilistic terms and, more specifically, be accounted for in harmony with Bayesian approaches to epistemology.[64] Interestingly for our present discussion, it is a basic assumption in Bayesian epistemology that one's degrees of belief should be updated by modifying one's existing set of credences in such a way (and not more than to the extent) that new beliefs form a coherent system together with the new ones. Remarkably, exactly the same dynamics is taken for granted in the completely different domain of the logic of belief revision (Gärdenfors 1988; Gärdenfors and Makinson 1988), where again it is a fundamental postulate that the update of one's belief set should not only be successful in terms of coherence of the new set, but also be minimal in the sense of leading to the loss of as few previous beliefs as possible. Epistemic agents should, in other words, give up beliefs only when forced to do so, and should then give up as few of them as possible.[65] The relevance of this with respect to the abovementioned virtue of conservativeness/minimisation of established beliefs is apparent: with the right tools, it might become possible to distinguish clearly between cases in which the conservation of certain established beliefs is justified all things considered, and cases in which instead it is merely motivated by a subjective attachment to the beliefs in question.[66]

On a related note, the virtue of *non-ad-hocness* might also be made more precise. Ad hocness indicates the fact that certain additional assumptions are made in a given theoretical context exclusively in order to save a certain belief, hypothesis of framework that would otherwise have to be abandoned in light of

---

[63] As we have seen, this is explicitly stated by at least some naturalists about metaphysics. Besides Harman (1965) and McMullin (1992, 1996) the locus classicus here is Lipton (2004). See also Day and Kincaid (1994), Aliseda (2006), McCain and Poston (2017) Schurz (2017), Douven (2017, 2022) and Magnani and Bertolotti (2017, parts B and C).

[64] See Hartmann and Sprenger (2011) for an overview of Bayesian epistemology, and Climenhaga (2017) and Douven and Schupbach (2015) for recent discussions of non-Bayesian renderings of inference to the best explanation.

[65] For more details, see Hansson (2011), but also the more critical Rott (2001).

[66] Obviously enough, an objective measure of the 'weight' of the various beliefs would then be required, which is by no means a small desideratum.

new relevant information in that context.[67] Wilcox (2023), for instance, provides a rigorous Bayesian account of successful accommodation as opposed to ad hocness in scientific theorising, which seems potentially applicable to metaphysics and the metaphysics of science as well.

In general, then, those undertaking the ambitious route of making theory choice in metaphysics (and science) rigorous, and ultimately vindicate the activity of at least some metaphysicians as functional to the discovery of fundamental truths about reality, should aim to define precise conceptual and formal instruments for integrating the novel indications coming from the sciences, the results of the analysis of possibilities carried out by metaphysicians, and the largely conservative belief system that we call 'common sense'.[68]

Let us move now to the second route that, as mentioned earlier, is available to metaphysicians who are aware of the complex set of issues surrounding theory choice in metaphysics and aim to gain some progress in this respect. In view of the important difficulties raised by the highly abstract nature of metaphysical questions and hypotheses, and of the ensuing problems in the evaluation and selection of theoretical alternatives, it will now be suggested, it is also a live option to reconceive – at least partly – metaphysics itself.

In a previous footnote, we mentioned Lipton's authoritative work on inference to the best explanation (2004). There, a distinction is drawn between *likely* explanations and *lovely* explanations – the former being more probably true than others, the latter being preferable to the alternatives on grounds that need not include truth or approximate truth. Given the customary conception of metaphysics as the inquiry into the fundamental structure of reality, it seems almost a truism that credible metaphysical hypotheses must be likely in Lipton's sense. Natural as the idea that metaphysical hypotheses must have a high level of likeliness may be, however, it is far from obvious that this is the only viable option. First of all, at a general level, while it seems indisputable that human subjects tend to believe in the truth of the explanatory hypotheses they employ, strictly speaking truth is not necessary for such use. Not only can one be a sceptic in general about the capability of our conjectures, hypotheses and theories to latch onto the true joints of reality, yet firmly believe in their usefulness. It also seems fair to say that the rationality of one's preference for

---

[67] Slightly differently, Schindler (2018, 132–133) puts forward a conception of ad hocness in terms of lack of coherence of a given hypothesis with the initial theory as well as with background theories.

[68] Along the way, further avenues of research could be explored in connection to metaphysics: for instance, the modelling of actual human reasoning in real-life situations, possibly also in association to potential applications in Artificial-Intelligence-related domains (on this, see for instance Flach and Kakas 2000); and the significance and potential usefulness of machine learning and automated discovery in the philosophy of science (see Williamson 2010).

a certain hypothesis based on the thought that it was overall better than the alternatives would (or at least could) remain untouched by the subsequent discovery that the selected hypothesis was false. If this, broadly Popperian, insight is correct, it follows that it is entirely rational to seek lovely explanations, and perhaps loveliness is all that we can aim for in view of underdetermination and the essential fallibility of our quest for knowledge.

Crucially for present purposes, this entails that in metaphysics there might be something more, or maybe something different, to theory choice than just truth or truth-likeness. It could be the case, in particular, that, in spite of the way the discipline has been conceived of historically, and is customarily defined and presented, metaphysical theory choice boils down to selecting the best means to achieve certain other goals – for instance, understanding, unified representation, or even just gratification through the creation of a complex mental construction that is in harmony with the observed facts. The option consequently emerges of exploring the possibility and prospects of a non-realist, yet non-eliminativist approach to metaphysics. Such an approach would move away from the usual characterisation of metaphysics, replacing it with something like Rosen's fictionalism about metaphysics (Rosen 2020), Godfrey-Smith's view of metaphysics as modelling without necessary ontological import (2006), McSweeney's reading of metaphysics as an essentially imaginative activity (2023) or Bueno's neo-Pyrrhonism (Bueno 2021, 2023). According to a fictionalist, for instance, metaphysicians may even play the 'truth game' when working on a particular hypothesis, but it is in fact not essential for the meaningfulness of their activity that it aim at the truth – even less that it be shown to be capable of attaining it.[69] Godfrey-Smith says something similar in terms of model-building and human explanatory practices. As for Bueno's views, the idea is that a 'positive' scepticism can be endorsed, according to which one may at the same time believe that there are no compelling reasons for certain ontological commitments and accept them and the theories that lead to them because doing so yields gains of a non-alethic nature – again, in terms of understanding, becoming aware of possible ways things could be like, satisfaction for the creation of grand conceptual schemes and so on.[70]

From this deflationist perspective on metaphysics, obviously enough, theoretical virtues may well be regarded as having an essentially pragmatic, rather than epistemic, value, also (or, especially) when it comes to devising very

---

[69] An interesting analogy can be drawn here with the different attitudes of experimental physicists working in laboratories, who are likely to at least implicitly assume a realist attitude towards the entities and processes that they believe to be studying, and theoretical physicists, who devise general theoretical frameworks and which do not demand realism, and who in fact – in several if not most cases – are not realists about their own constructions.

[70] The possibility to endorse what she calls 'pragmatism' about metaphysics is discussed and explicitly accepted as a consistent form of non-eliminative naturalism by Emery (2023).

abstract descriptions of reality such as those that are routinely put forward by metaphysicians (on this, see Nolan 2014). This would make arguments against explanationism in metaphysics – such as those put forward by Saatsi and Ladyman, which we mentioned earlier – lose a lot of their force. A deflationist/fictionalist attitude towards metaphysics could also block the sort of criticism raised by McKenzie (2020). McKenzie points out that, even assuming that some form of naturalistic metaphysics is preferable to traditional metaphysics of the anti-naturalistic type, an important problem remains. For, she points out, our best science is very likely to be incomplete, and our current theories destined to be replaced by rather different ones. Moreover, some of the theories that we currently accept are internally inconsistent (as in the case of the 'bare' quantum mechanics we have discussed a few pages back), and some mutually incompatible (as in the case of relativity and quantum theory, which are very successful in their respective domains, yet cannot be put together in their current form so as to provide an all-embracing description of reality, valid at all scales). According to McKenzie, while this doesn't diminish the value of science, it raises serious worries about the usefulness of metaphysics, even in a naturalistic formulation of it. For, again, the significance of science does not depend on the truth of the theories that we employ beyond the phenomena (it is for this very reason that naturalists can coherently be scientific antirealists). Metaphysics, instead, says McKenzie, has truth as an essential aim and cannot consequently be informed by incomplete, or even contradictory and/or inconsistent theories. In other words, there is no space for approximation in metaphysics, hence science-based metaphysics should in fact wait for the final scientific theory (or theories). Things change radically, however, if – a possibility that, incidentally, McKenzie explicitly mentions in her paper – truth is replaced by something different as the aim of metaphysics. For instance, the fact that one seeks understanding via metaphysical concepts and categories on the basis of successful, yet incomplete and mutually incompatible, scientific theories sounds perfectly acceptable in a fictionalist context.[71]

Of course, the issue remains of how to bring theoretical virtues to bear on theory choice, especially if – as suggested earlier – general criteria are lacking for defining objective 'rankings'. If theoretical virtues need not be regarded as truth-conducive, however, a more relaxed, pluralist approach is admissible. For instance, an approach whereby the comparative assessment of various theories in relation to their empirical and non-empirical virtues is based on something like 'reflective equilibrium' (Rawls 1971; Daniels 2020). That is, on

---

[71] For a related discussion of theoretical virtues and truth, see Hildebrand (2023), especially section 8.

a subjective and context-dependent evaluation of the theory in connection to other beliefs, where the entire set of beliefs is appraised and revised until we obtain an acceptable coherent set.[72]

4.3 Summary and Assessment

In conclusion, as soon as one examines the way in which scientific theories and metaphysical hypotheses interact, especially when it comes to building integrated models of reality that encompass both science and metaphysics, one realises the need to carefully examine the very nature of the form(s) of reasoning involved in our explanatory practices. Especially so, when reflection on theoretical virtues as 'tie-breakers' among different explanatory hypotheses that are equally compatible with the empirical data is concerned. Indeed, in both metaphysics and the sciences ampliative reasoning is involved, in the form of abductive inferences that, inevitably, take non-empirical factors into account. In view of this, existing work on abduction/inference to the best explanation on the one hand, and on theoretical virtues in metaphysics and science on the other could certainly, and in fact should, be integrated and expanded in new directions. The more ambitious goal of showing that realism in metaphysics is as justified as in science may, however, eventually be replaced by a deflationary conception of metaphysics as seeking understanding (or something else) rather than truth.

5 Concluding Outline

Assuming that in the majority of cases it is uncontroversial whether one is dealing with science or metaphysics (or neither), several questions emerge as soon as one looks at their mutual relationship. First and foremost, questions concerning the methodology of metaphysics in connection to the sciences. In the more or less recent history of philosophy, various positions and approaches have been defined with respect to this. Nowadays, it seems hard to deny that metaphysicians should pay attention to the indications coming from science.

---

[72] This has an obvious connection with the above discussion of Bayesian updating and belief revision. To avoid misunderstanding, while it fits a generally pragmatist attitude towards explanatory hypotheses and their comparative assessment, reflective equilibrium is also perfectly compatible with an approach that takes non-empirical theoretical virtues to point towards the truth. In relation to this, it is worth mentioning once more Chakravartty (2017), where a clearly non-epistemic interpretation of theoretical virtues is put forward, together with an emphasis on explanatory power. Chakravartty, in particular, combines scientific realism with a voluntarist epistemology that allows for variation of ontological commitments across different rational inquirers, whose underlying commitments are defined on the basis of subjective choices. This means, among other things, that whether and to what extent theoretical virtues are considered truth-conducive depends on subjective views on the amount of epistemic risk it appears reasonable to take.

This means to endorse some form of ontological and/or methodological naturalism. In this Element, we have looked in some detail at the issue of naturalism in connection to metaphysics, suggesting a taxonomy of various views ranging from radical anti-naturalism to radical naturalism. We then emphasised the highly under-determined nature of metaphysical explanations: no matter how intimately with our best current science one develops their metaphysics, several conceptual alternatives seem always available. And it is far from easy to determine the criteria which should be employed for evaluating the various options. A further examination of the issue of theory choice in metaphysics, we therefore concluded, is the most pressing methodological problem for the discipline. Exploring this area of research, we suggested in closing, may even lead to a deep reconceptualisation of metaphysics itself, especially in connection to scientific inquiry. In the course of the discussion, we looked at some case studies involving metaphysical concepts and hypotheses as well as scientific evidence and theories. Besides providing a more concrete illustration of the interplay between metaphysics and the sciences, these examples also offered a clear illustration of the plausibility and significance of approaches to metaphysics that, while acknowledging that science may in many cases provide essential input and insights, refuse to give up the autonomy of metaphysics.

References

Aliseda, A., (2006): *Abductive Reasoning: Logical Investigations into Discovery and Explanation*, Synthese Library 330, Dordrecht, Springer.

Alspector-Kelly, M., (2001): *On Quine on Carnap on Ontology*, Philosophical Studies, 102, 93–122.

Balaguer, M., (2010): *Free Will as an Open Scientific Problem*, Cambridge, Massachusetts, MIT Press.

Bealer, G., (1998): *Intuition and the Autonomy of Philosophy*, in DePaul, M. and Ramsey, W. (eds.), 201–240.

Bealer, G., (1996): *A Priori Knowledge and the Scope of Philosophy*, Philosophical Studies, 81, 121–142.

Bigaj, T., (2022): *Identity and Indiscernibility in Quantum Mechanics*, Switzerland, Palgrave Macmillan.

Bird, A. and Tobin, E., (2023): *Natural Kinds*, in Zalta, E. N. and Nodelman, U. (eds.), *The Stanford Encyclopedia of Philosophy* (Spring 2023 Edition), https://plato.stanford.edu/archives/spr2023/entries/natural-kinds/.

Bonjour, L., (1998): *In Defense of Pure Reason*, Cambridge, Cambridge University Press.

Boyd, R., (1999): *Homeostasis, Species, and Higher Taxa*, in Wilson, R. (ed.), *Species: New Interdisciplinary Essays*, Cambridge, Massachusetts, MIT Press, 141–186.

Braddon-Mitchell, D. and Nola, R. (eds.), (2009): *Conceptual Analysis and Philosophical Naturalism*, Cambridge, Massachusetts, MIT Press.

Brenner, A., (2017): *Simplicity as a Criterion of Theory Choice in Metaphysics*, Philosophical Studies, 174, 2687–2707.

Bryant, A., (2020): *Keep the Chickens Cooped: The Epistemic Inadequacy of Free Range Metaphysics*, Synthese, 197, 1867–1887.

Bueno, O., (2023): *Dispensing with Facts, Substances and Structures*, American Philosophical Quarterly, 60, 49–61.

Bueno, O., (2021): *Neo-Pyrrhonism, Empiricism, and Scientific Activity*, Veritas, 1, 1–14.

Bueno, O. and Shalkowski, S. A., (2020): *Troubles with Theoretical Virtues: Resisting Theoretical Utility Arguments in Metaphysics*, Philosophy and Phenomenological Research, 101, 2, 456–469.

Callender, C., (2011): *Philosophy of Science and Metaphysics*. In French, S. and Saatsi, J. (eds.), *The Continuum Companion to the Philosophy of Science*, London, Continuum, 33–54.

Calosi, C. and Mariani, C., (2021): *Quantum Indeterminacy*, Philosophy Compass, 16, 4, e12731.

Carnap, R., (1950): *Empiricism, Semantics, and Ontology*, Revue Internationale De Philosophie, 4, 20–40. English translation in Carnap, R., (1967): *The Logical Structure of the World and Pseudoproblems in Philosophy*, Translated by George, R. A., Berkeley and Los Angeles, University of California Press.

Chakravartty, A., (2017): *Scientific Ontology: Integrating Naturalized Metaphysics and Voluntarist Epistemology*, Oxford, Oxford University Press.

Chakravartty, A., (2017a): *Scientific Realism*, in Zalta, E. N. (ed.), *The Stanford Encyclopedia of Philosophy*, https://plato.stanford.edu/archives/sum2017/entries/scientific-realism/.

Chakravartty, A., (2013): *On the Prospects of Naturalized Metaphysics*, in Ross, D., Ladyman, J. and Kincaid, H. (eds.), 27–50.

Chakravartty, A., (2007): *A Metaphysics for Scientific Realism*, Cambridge, Cambridge University Press.

Climenhaga, N., (2017): *Inference to the Best Explanation Made Incoherent*, Journal of Philosophy, 14, 251–273.

Cooper, R., (2012): *Is Psychiatric Classification a Good Thing?* in Kendler, K. S. and Parnas, J. (eds.), *Philosophical Issues in Psychiatry II: Nosology*, Oxford, Oxford University Press, 61–70.

Cowling, S., (2013): *Ideological Parsimony*, Synthese, 190, 3889–3908.

Crisp, T., (2016): *On Naturalistic Metaphysics*, in Clark, K. J. (ed.), *The Blackwell Companion to Naturalism*, Hoboken, New Jersey, John Wiley and Sons, 61–74.

Daniels, N., (2020): *Reflective Equilibrium*, in Zalta, E. N. (ed.), *The Stanford Encyclopedia of Philosophy*, https://plato.stanford.edu/archives/sum2020/entries/reflective-equilibrium/.

Day, T. and Kincaid, H., (1994): *Putting Inference to the Best Explanation in Its Place*, Synthese, 98, 271–295.

De Caro, M. and Macarthur, D., (2004): *Introduction* to De Caro, M. and Macarthur, D. (eds.), *Naturalism in Question*, Cambridge, Massachusetts, Harvard University Press, 1–18.

De Caro, M. and Voltolini, A., (2010): *Is Liberal Naturalism Possible?* in De Caro, M. and Macarthur, D. (eds.), *Naturalism and Normativity*, New York, Columbia University Press, 69–86.

DePaul, M. R. and Ramsey, W. M., (eds.) (1998): *Rethinking Intuition: The Psychology of Intuition and its Role in Philosophical Inquiry*. Maryland, Rowman & Littlefield Publishers.

Douglas, H., (2013): *The Value of Cognitive Values*, Philosophy of Science, 80, 5, 796–806.

Douven, I., (2022): *The Art of Abduction*, Cambridge, Massachusetts Institute of Technology Press.

Douven, I., (2017): *Abduction*, in Edward, N. Zalta (ed.), *The Stanford Encyclopedia of Philosophy* (Summer 2017 Edition), https://plato.stanford .edu/archives/sum2017/entries/abduction/.

Douven, I. and Schupbach, J., (2015): *Probabilistic Alternatives to Bayesianism: The Case of Explanationism*, Frontiers in Psychology, 6, 1–9.

Duprè, J., (1993): *The Disorder of Things: Metaphysical Foundations of the Disunity of Science*, Cambridge, Massachussetts, Harvard University Press.

Ellis, G., (2016): *How Can Physics Underlie the Mind?* Berlin, Springer-Verlag.

Emery, N., (2023): *Naturalism Beyond the Limits of Science*, New York, Oxford University Press.

Engelhard, K., Feldbacher-Escamilla, C. J., Gebharter, A. and Seide, A., (2021): *Inductive Metaphysics*, Grazer Philosophische Studien, 98.

Evans, G., (1978): *Can there be Vague Objects?*, *Analysis*, 38 (4), 208.

Flach, P. A. and Kakas, A. C. (eds.), (2000): *Abduction and Induction*, Dordrecht, Kluwer.

French, S., (2019): *Identity and Individuality in Quantum Theory*, in Zalta, E. N. (ed.), *The Stanford Encyclopedia of Philosophy* (Winter 2019 Edition), https://plato.stanford.edu/archives/win2019/entries/qt-idind/.

French, S., (2014): *The Structure of the World: Metaphysics and Representation*, Oxford, Oxford University Press.

French, S. and Krause, D., (1995): *Vague Identity and Quantum Non-individuality*, Analysis, 55, 1, 20–26.

French, S. and McKenzie, K., (2015): *Rethinking Outside the Toolbox: Reflecting Again on the Relationship between Philosophy of Science and Metaphysics*, in Bigaj, T. and Wüthrich, C. (eds.), *Metaphysics in Contemporary Physics*, Amsterdam, Brill, 25–54.

French, S. and McKenzie, K., (2012): *Thinking Outside the Toolbox: Towards a More Productive Engagement between Metaphysics and Philosophy of Physics*, European Journal of Analytic Philosophy, 8, 1, 42–59.

Gärdenfors, P. and Makinson, D., (1988): *Revisions of Knowledge Systems Using Epistemic Entrenchment*, Proceedings of the Second Conference on Theoretical Aspects of Reasoning about Knowledge, San Francisco, California, Morgan Kaufmann, 83–95.

Ginet, C., (1966): *Might We Have No Choice?*, in Lehrer, K. (ed.), *Freedom and Determinism*, New York, Random House, 87–104.

Godfrey-Smith, P., (2006): *Theories and Models in Metaphysics*, Harvard Review of Philosophy, 14, 4–19.

Goldman, A. I., (2015): *Naturalizing Metaphysics with the Help of Cognitive Science*, in Bennett, K. and Zimmerman, D. W. (eds.), *Oxford Studies in Metaphysics*, vol. 9, Oxford, Oxford University Press, 171–215.

Goldman, A. I., (2007): *A Program for 'Naturalizing' Metaphysics, with Application to the Ontology of Events*, The Monist, 90, 457–479.

Goldman, A. I. and McLaughlin, B. P. (eds.), (2019): *Metaphysics and Cognitive Science*, New York, Oxford University Press.

Hacking, I., (2007): *Natural Kinds: Rosy Dawn, Scholastic Twilight*, Royal Institute of Philosophy Supplement, 61, 203–239.

Haji, I., (1999): *Indeterminism and Frankfurt-Type Examples*, Philosophical Explorations, 1, 42–58.

Hansson, S. O., (2011): *Logic of Belief Revision*, in Zalta, E. N. (ed.), *The Stanford Encyclopedia of Philosophy* (Fall 2011 Edition), https://plato.stan ford.edu/archives/fall2011/entries/logic-belief-revision/.

Harman, G., (1965): *The Inference to the Best Explanation*, Philosophical Review, 74, 88–95.

Hartmann, S. and Sprenger, J., (2011): *Bayesian Epistemology*, in Pritchard, D. and Bernecker, S. (eds.), *The Routledge Companion to Epistemology*, London, Routledge, 609–620.

Held, C., (2022): *The Kochen-Specker Theorem*, in Zalta, E. N. and Nodelman, U. (eds.): *The Stanford Encyclopedia of Philosophy*, https://plato.stanford .edu/archives/fall2022/entries/kochen-specker/.

Hildebrand, T., (2023): *Laws of Nature*, Cambridge, Cambridge University Press.

Hudson, H., (2016): *Non-naturalistic Metaphysics*, in Clark, K. J. (ed.), *The Blackwell Companion to Naturalism*, Hoboken, New Jersey, John Wiley and Sons, 168–181.

Humphreys, P., (2013): *Speculative Ontology*, in Ross, D., Ladyman, J. and Kincaid, H. (eds.), 51–78.

Husserl, E., (1970[1936]): *The Crisis of European Sciences and Transcendental Phenomenology*, translated by Carr, D., Evaston, Illinois, Northwestern University Press.

Hylton, P., (1994): *Quine's Naturalism*, Midwest Studies in Philosophy, 19, 261–282.

Jansson, L. and Tallant, J., (2017): *Quantitative Parsimony: Probably for the Better*, British Journal for the Philosophy of Science, 68, 781–803.

Kane, R., (1996): *The Significance of Free Will*, New York, Oxford University Press.

Keas, M. N., (2018): *Systematizing Theoretical Virtues*, Synthese, 195, 2761–2793.

Khalidi, M. A., (2013): *Natural Categories and Human Kinds: Classification in the Natural and Social Sciences*, Cambridge, Cambridge University Press.

Kim, J., (2011): *From Naturalism to Physicalism: Supervenience Redux*, Proceedings and Addresses of the American Philosophical Association, 85, 2, 109–134.

Kornblith, H., (1998): *The Role of Intuition in Philosophical Inquiry: An Account with No Unnatural Ingredients*, in DePaul, M. and Ramsey, W. (eds.), 129–142.

Kuhn, T. S., (1977): *Objectivity, Value Judgment, and Theory Choice*, in Kuhn, T. S. (ed.), *The Essential Tension*, Chicago, Illinois, University of Chicago Press, 320–339.

Ladyman, J., (2017): *An Apology for Naturalized Metaphysics*, in Slater, M. and Yudell, Z. (eds.), 141–162.

Ladyman, J., (2012): *Science, Metaphysics and Method*, Philosophical Studies, 160, 31–51.

Ladyman, J. and Ross, D. (with Spurrett, D. and Collier, J.), (2007): *Every Thing Must Go. Metaphysics Naturalised*, Oxford, Oxford University Press.

Lewis, D., (1986): *On the Plurality of Worlds*, Oxford, Blackwell.

Libet, B., (2002): *Do We Have Free Will?* in Kane, R. (ed.), *Oxford Handbook of Free Will*, New York, Oxford University Press, 551–564.

Lipton, P., (2004): *Inference to the Best Explanation*, (second edition), London, Routledge.

Lowe, E. J., (2011): *The Possibility of Metaphysics: Substance, Identity, and Time*, Oxford, Oxford University Press.

Lowe, E. J., (2007): *The Four-Category Ontology: A Metaphysical Foundation for Natural Science*, Oxford, Oxford University Press.

Lowe, E. J., (1994): *Vague Identity and Quantum Indeterminacy*, Analysis, 54, 2, 110–114.

Macarthur, D., (2019): *Liberal Naturalism and the Scientific Image of the World*, Inquiry: An Interdisciplinary Journal of Philosophy, 62, 5, 565–585.

Mackonis, A., (2013): *Inference to the Best Explanation, Coherence and Other Explanatory Virtues*, Synthese, 190, 6, 975–995.

Maclaurin, J. and Dyke, H., (2012): *What Is Analytic Metaphysics For?* Australasian Journal of Philosophy, 90, 291–306.

Maddy, P., (2007): *Second Philosophy: A Naturalistic Method*, Oxford, Oxford University Press.

Magnani, L. and Bertolotti, T. (eds.), (2017): *Springer Handbook of Model-Based Science*, Dordrecht, Springer.

Mallon, D., (2006): *Race: Normative, Not Metaphysical or Semantic*, Ethics, 116, 33, 525–551.

Maudlin, T., (2007): *The Metaphysics within Physics*, Oxford, Oxford University Press.

McCain, K. and Poston, T. (eds.), (2017): *Best Explanations*, Oxford, Oxford University Press.

McKenzie, K., (2020): *A Curse on Both Houses: Naturalistic versus a Priori Metaphysics and the Problem of Progress*, Res Philosophica, 97, 1, 1–29.

McLeod, M. and Parsons, J., (2013): *Maclaurin and Dyke on Analytic Metaphysics*, Australasian Journal of Philosophy, 91, 173–178.

McMullin, E., (2014): *The Virtues of a Good Theory*, in Curd, M. and Psillos, S. (eds.), *The Routledge Companion to Philosophy of Science*, New York, Routledge, 561–571.

McMullin, E., (1996): *Epistemic Virtue and Theory-Appraisal*, in Douven, I. and Horsten, L. (eds.), *Realism in the Sciences*, Leuven, Leuven University Press, 1–34.

McMullin, E., (1992): *The Inference that Makes Science*, Milwaukee, Wisconsin, Marquette University Press.

McSweeney, M. M., (2023): *Metaphysics as Essentially Imaginative and Aiming at Understanding*, American Philosophical Quarterly, 60, 83–97.

Melnyk, A., (2013): *Can Metaphysics Be Naturalized? And, if So, How?* in Ross, D., Ladyman, J. and Kincaid, H. (eds.), 79–95.

Miller, K. and Norton, J., (2022): *Everyday Metaphysical Explanation*, Oxford, Oxford University Press.

Mohammadian, M., (2017): *Theoretical Virtues in Science and in Metaphysics*, PhD Thesis, University of Notre Dame.

Morganti, M., (2022): *Liberal Naturalism, Ontological Commitment and Explanation*, in De Caro, M. and Macarthur, D. (eds.), *The Routledge Handbook of Liberal Naturalism*, Oxford, Routledge, 245–254.

Morganti, M., (2020a): *Fundamentality in Metaphysics and the Philosophy of Physics. Part I: Metaphysics*, Philosophy Compass, 15 (7).

Morganti, M., (2020b): *Fundamentality in Metaphysics and the Philosophy of Physics. Part II: The Philosophy of Physics*, Philosophy Compass, 15 (10).

Morganti, M., (2013): *Combining Science and Metaphysics: Contemporary Physics, Conceptual Revision and Common Sense*, Basingstoke, Palgrave Macmillan.

Morganti, M. and Tahko, T. E., (2017): *Moderately Naturalistic Metaphysics*, Synthese, 194, 2557–2580.

Moore, G. E., (1959): *Philosophical Papers*. London: Allen & Unwin.

Nahmias, E., (2014): *Is Free Will an Illusion? Confronting Challenges from the Modern Mind Sciences*, in Sinnott-Armstrong, W. (ed.), *Moral Psychology*

(Volume 4: Free Will and Moral Responsibility), Cambridge, Massachusetts, MIT Press, 1–25.

Neta, R., (2007): Review of De Caro, M. and Macarthur, D. (eds.), *Naturalism in Question*, The Philosophical Review, 116, 657–663.

Nolan, D., (2014): *The Dangers of Pragmatic Virtue*, Inquiry: An Interdisciplinary Journal of Philosophy, 57, 623–644.

Nolan, D., (1997): *Quantitative Parsimony*, British Journal for the Philosophy of Science, 48, 329–343.

Norton, J., (2021): *Material Induction*, Calgary, University of Calgary Press.

Okasha, S., (2011): *Theory Choice and Social Choice: Kuhn Versus Arrow*, Mind, 120, 83–115.

Oppenheim, P. and Putnam, H., (1958): *The Unity of Science as a Working Hypothesis*, Minnesota Studies in the Philosophy of Science, 2, 3–36.

Paul, L. A., (2012): *Metaphysics as Modeling: The Handmaiden's Tale*, Philosophical Studies, 160, 1–29.

Plantinga, A., (2002): *Introduction and Final Replies to Commentators*, in Beilby, J. (ed.), *Naturalism Defeated? Essays on Plantinga's Evolutionary Argument against Naturalism*, Ithaca, New York, Cornell, 1–12 and 204–276.

Price, H. (2007): *Quining Naturalism*, Journal of Philosophy, 104 (8), 375–402.

Pust, J., (2019): *Intuition*, in Zalta, E. N. (ed.), *The Stanford Encyclopedia of Philosophy*, https://plato.stanford.edu/archives/sum2019/entries/intuition/.

Pust, J., (2000): *Intuition as Evidence*, New York, Routledge.

Putnam, H., (2004): *Ethics without Ontology*, Cambridge, Massachusetts, Harvard University Press.

Quine, W. v. O., (1981): *Theories and Things*, Cambridge, Massachusetts, Harvard University Press.

Quine, W. v. O., (1951): *On Carnap's Views on Ontology*, Philosophical Studies, 2, 65–72.

Quine, W. v. O. and Ullian, J. S., (1978): *The Web of Belief*, New York, McGraw-Hill.

Rawls, J., (1971): *A Theory of Justice*, Cambridge, Massachusetts, Harvard University Press.

Ritchie, J., (2008): *Understanding Naturalism*, Durham, Acumen.

Rose, D. (ed.), (2017): *Experimental Metaphysics*, New York, Bloomsbury.

Rosen, G., (2020): *Metaphysics as a Fiction*, in Armour-Garb, B. and Kroon, F. (eds.), *Fictionalism in Philosophy*, Oxford, Oxford University Press, 28–47.

Rosen, G., (2014): *Quine and the Revival of Metaphysics*, in Harman, G. and Lepore, E. (eds.), *A Companion to W.v.O. Quine*, Oxford, John Wiley and Sons, 552–570.

Roskies, A., (2014): *Can Neuroscience Resolve Issues about Free Will?* in Sinnott-Armstrong, W. (ed.), *Moral Psychology* (Volume 4: Free Will and Moral Responsibility), Cambridge, Massachusetts, MIT Press, 103–126.

Ross, D., Ladyman, J. and Kincaid, H. (eds.), (2013): *Scientific Metaphysics*, Oxford, Oxford University Press.

Rott, H., (2001): *Change, Choice and Inference: A Study of Belief Revision and Nonmonotonic Reasoning*, Oxford, Clarendon Press.

Saatsi, J., (2017): *Explanation and Explanationism in Science and Metaphysics*, in Slater, M. and Yudell, Z. (eds.), 162–191.

Schaffer, J., (2009): *On What Grounds What*, in Manley, D., Chalmers, D. and Wasserman, R. (eds.), *Metametaphysics: New Essays on the Foundations of Ontology*, Oxford, Oxford University Press, 347–383.

Schindler, S., (2022): *Theoretical Virtues: Do Scientists Think What Philosophers Think They Ought to Think?* Philosophy of Science, 89, 524–564.

Schindler, S., (2018): *Theoretical Virtues in Science: Uncovering Reality through Theory*, Cambridge, Cambridge University Press.

Schurger, A., Hu, P., Pak, J. and Roskies, A., (2021): *What Is the Readiness Potential?* Trends in Cognitive Sciences, 25, 7, 558–570.

Schurz, G., (2021): *Abduction as a Method of Inductive Metaphysics*, Grazer Philosophische Studien, 98, 50–74.

Schurz, G., (2017): *Patterns of Abductive Inference*, in Magnani, L. and Bortolotti, T. (eds.), 151–173.

Sellars, W. S., (1962): *Philosophy and the Scientific Image of Man*, in Colodny, R. (ed.), *Frontiers of Science and Philosophy*, Pittsburgh, Pennsylvania, University of Pittsburgh Press, 1–40.

Shimony, A., (1981): *Critique of the Papers of Fine and Suppes*, Philosophy of Science, Proceedings 1980, 2, 572–580.

Slater, M. and Yudell, Z. (eds.), (2017): *Metaphysics and the Philosophy of Science: New Essays*, Oxford, Oxford University Press.

Sober, E., (2022): *Parsimony Arguments in Science and Metaphysics, and Their Connection with Unification, Fundamentality, and Epistemological Holism*, in Ioannidis, S., Vishne, G., Hemmo, M. and Shenker, O. (eds.), *Levels of Reality in Science and Philosophy: Re-examining the Multi-level Structure of Reality*, Switzerland, Springer International, 229–260.

Sober, E., (2015): *Ockham's Razor: A User's Manual*, Cambridge, Cambridge University Press.

Sober, E., (2009): *Parsimony Arguments in Science and Philosophy – A Test Case for Naturalism*, Proceedings and Addresses of the American Philosophical Association, 83, 117–155.

Spencer, Q., (2018): *Racial Realism I: Are Biological Races Real?* Philosophy Compass, 13, 1, e12468.

Spencer, Q., (2018a): *Racial Realism II: Are Folk Races Real?* Philosophy Compass, 13, 1, e12467.

Stegenga, J., (2015): *Theory Choice and Social Choice: Okasha versus Sen*, Mind, 124, 263–277.

Stoljar, D., (2023): *Physicalism*, in Zalta, E. N. (ed.), *The Stanford Encyclopedia of Philosophy*, https://plato.stanford.edu/archives/sum2023/entries/physicalism/.

Strawson, P. F., (1959): *Individuals: An Essay in Descriptive Metaphysics*, London, Routledge.

Tahko, T. E., (2018): *Fundamentality*, in Zalta, E. N. (ed.), The Stanford Encyclopedia of Philosophy (Fall 2018 Edition), https://plato.stanford.edu/archives/fall2018/entries/fundamentality/.

Thagard, P. R., (1978): *The Best Explanation: Criteria for Theory Choice*, The Journal of Philosophy, 75, 76–92.

Torza, A., (2023): *Indeterminacy in the World*, Cambridge, Cambridge University Press.

Ullmann-Margalit, E. and Morgenbesser, S., (1977): *Picking and Choosing*, Social Research: An International Quarterly, 44, 4, 757–785.

Van Fraassen, B. C., (2002): *The Empirical Stance*, New Haven, Connecticut, Yale University Press.

Van Fraassen, B. C., (1991): *Quantum Mechanics*, Oxford, Clarendon Press.

Van Fraassen, B. C., (1980): *The Scientific Image*, Oxford, Clarendon Press.

Van Fraassen, B. C., (1972): *A Formal Approach to the Philosophy of Science*, in Colodny, R. (ed.), *Paradigms and Paradoxes: The Philosophical Challenge of the Quantum Domain*, Pittsburgh, Pennsylvania, University of Pittsburgh Press, 303–366.

Van Inwagen, P., (1983): *An Essay on Free Will*, Oxford, Clarendon Press.

Wegner, D., (2002): *The Illusion of Conscious Will*, Cambridge, Massachusetts, MIT Press.

Wilcox, J., (2023): *Ad Hocness, Accomodation and Consilience: A Bayesian Account*, Synthese, 201 (2).

Williamson, J., (2010): *The Philosophy of Science in Relation to Machine Learning*, in Gaber, M. M. (ed.), *Scientific Data Mining and Knowledge Discovery: Principles and Foundations*, Berlin, Springer, 77–89.

Witmer, G., (2012): *Naturalism and Physicalism*, in Barnard, R. and Manson, N. (eds.), *Continuum Companion to Metaphysics*, New York, Bloomsbury, 90–120.

Acknowledgements

For useful discussions on various issues surrounding science and philosophy, I am grateful to Mario Alai, Raoni Arroyo, Mauro Dorato and Emanuele Rossanese. Samuel Schindler provided invaluable help by reading the entire manuscript in one of its previous forms and making a number of very useful suggestions. This project has been partially supported by the Italian Ministry of University and Research through two national research grants – PRIN 2017 project "The Manifest Image and the Scientific Image" prot. 2017ZNWW7F_003 and PRIN 2020 project prot. 20224HXFLY. It was also partially supported on the basis of Portuguese national funds by FCT – Fundação para a Ciência e a Tecnologia, I.P., under the PHI-ASM Project – Philosophical Investigation of Applications of Science in Mathematics, reference PeX.2022.06784.PTDC. DOI: http://doi.org/10.54499/2022.06784.PTDC.

Cambridge Elements ☰

Metaphysics

Tuomas E. Tahko
University of Bristol

Tuomas E. Tahko is Professor of Metaphysics of Science at the University of Bristol, UK. Tahko specializes in contemporary analytic metaphysics, with an emphasis on methodological and epistemic issues: 'meta-metaphysics'. He also works at the interface of metaphysics and philosophy of science: 'metaphysics of science'. Tahko is the author of *Unity of Science* (Cambridge University Press, 2021), *An Introduction to Metametaphysics* (Cambridge University Press, 2015) and editor of *Contemporary Aristotelian Metaphysics* (Cambridge University Press, 2012).

About the Series

This highly accessible series of Elements provides brief but comprehensive introductions to the most central topics in metaphysics. Many of the Elements also go into considerable depth, so the series will appeal to both students and academics. Some Elements bridge the gaps between metaphysics, philosophy of science, and epistemology.

Cambridge Elements ≡

Metaphysics

Elements in the Series

A full series listing is available at: www.cambridge.org/EMPH

Printed in the United States
by Baker & Taylor Publisher Services